AF220512

Cover pictures

Steamship America, used to immigrate by Johannes Würthner. Source: Kludas 1991, p. 13.

Newspaper ad, showing a timetable with Johannes Würthner's departure on 2nd of July, 1864. Source: *Aschaffenburger Zeitung*, 11th of June, 1864.

Immigrated
The Family Branch Würthner/Käfer

Bibliografische Information der Deutschen Bibliothek
Diese Publikation ist in der Deutschen Nationalbibliothek verzeichnet;
detaillierte bibliografische Angaben sind im Internet über
<http://dnb.nb.de> abrufbar.

© 2018 Stefan Matysiak
Herstellung und Verlag: BoD – Books on Demand, Norderstedt
Umschlagbild & Layout: Stefan Matysiak
matymedia.de

Das Werk einschließlich aller seiner Teile ist urheberrechtlich geschützt.
Jede Verwertung außerhalb der Grenzen des Urheberrechtsgesetzes ist
ohne Zustimmung unzulässig und strafbar.

ISBN 978-3-7528-7968-1

Table of Contents

The Emigration from Wuerttemberg to the US and the Wuerttemberg Press

Stefan Matysiak

When the family's ancestors, Johannes Würthner and Maria Käfer, left their hometown Schwenningen, the emigration of large parts of the population had already had a big effect on a long phase of the history of their independent Duchy of Wuerttemberg (since 1806 Kingdom of Wuerttemberg). Although many people emigrated from other German states, too, Wuerttemberg was a country with a particularly large number of emigrants.[1] In the 18th and 19th century, "no other region of mainland Europe experienced a similarly extensive emigration."[2] This emigration was supported by the fact that the Wuerttemberg constitution allowed every inhabitant to emigrate. Wuerttemberg was "until the middle of the 19th century one of the few German countries that did not complicate or even obstruct emigration".[3]

It could have been a mere coincidence that Johannes Würthner and Maria Käfer emigrated to the US, because they had many alternative destinations to choose from. At first, most of the Wuerttemberg people – called Swabians – migrated to southeastern Europe. Many of these desti-

---

[1] Cf. Maier 2004: 18.
[2] Scheuerbrandt 1985, p. 6.
[3] Scheuerbrandt 1985, p. 5.

nations belonged to Austria, a country, which was under rule of the dynasty of Hapsburg, the House of Austria. The Archduchy of Hapsburg (since 1804 Empire of Austria) started to extend to large parts of South East Europe since the end of the 15th century. Because large areas were uninhabited, the House of Hapsburg recruited German settlers.

Wuerttemberg Swabians in particular set off on their way and followed the Danube shores ("Danubian Swabian") towards Hungary, Croatia, Serbia, and Romania, where closed Swabian settlement areas emerged.[4] This emigration included many inhabitants of the county of Rottweil, to which Schwenningen belonged.[5] The Danube begins 9 miles south of Schwenningen, in Donaueschingen at the confluence of the rivers Brigach and Breg (see map pp. 10-11). Austrian Bohemia attracted many emigrants, too.[6]

At first, the Russian Empire was also a popular destination. Russia, like Austria, was seeking German settlers. The country promised the new citizens from Germany interest-free loans, tax exemption and self-government rights. While Wuerttemberg suffered from misery, the Russian offer had an "irresistible attraction".[7] Many Germans (at first from Bavaria, Baden, Hesse, the Palatinate and the Rhineland) settled in the Russian Volga region. At the very beginning of the 19th century, many Wuerttemberg settlers from the Ulm region followed to Russia.[8] In the Volga Region, the Black Sea area and in today's countries Czech Republic, Hungary, Romania, Ukraine and Georgia developed closed German and even Wuerttemberg settlement areas.[9]

Major waves of Wuerttemberg emigration

A first major wave of emigration, occurred in Wuerttemberg during the change from the 17th to the 18th century. At that time, especially people from the northern parts of the duchy, fled abroad. This region was particularly impoverished because, since the 17th century, the French army and various German troops had marched through it. The troops had plundered

---

[4] Cf. Maier 2004b, pp. 11/12.
[5] Cf. Maier 2004b, pp. 11/12.
[6] Cf. Hippel 1984, pp. 250/51.
[7] Ekbal 2006, p. 5.
[8] Cf. Hippel 1984, pp. 250/51.
[9] Cf. Maier 2004b, p. 11.

and raided the villages and towns regularly, so that the population was not able to recover and permanently starving.[10] From 1708 to 1709 there was also a "terribly hard winter",[11] which also affected the population badly and forced them to emigrate.

But most of the Swabians left their homeland in the 19th and not in the 18th century. Emigration did not administer evenly across the century, but there were significant peaks (see figure).

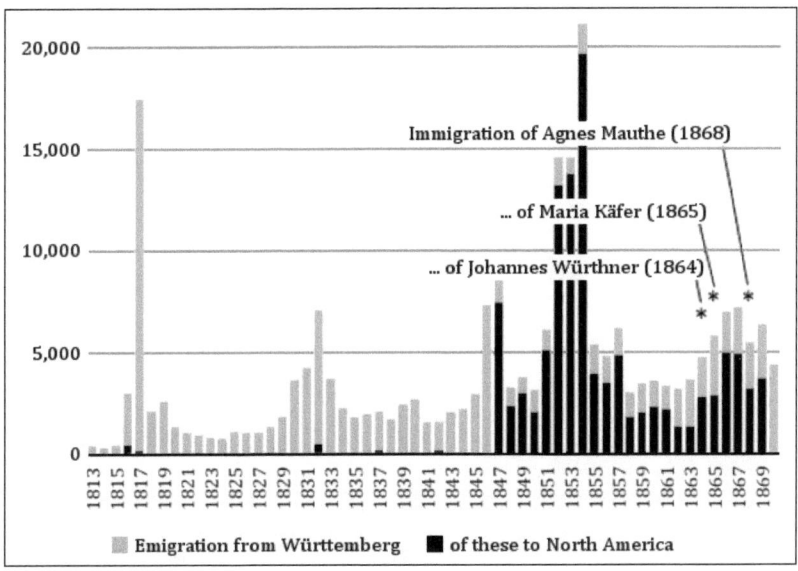

Figure: official emigration from Wuerttemberg.[12]

The first phase of a very strong emigration wave started in 1816, when southwestern Germany suffered from famine.[13] Already in the 17th and 18th century, Wuerttemberg had become the poorhouse of Europe. Wars and years of crop failures had impoverished large parts of the population. After 1816 things got worse. In Schwenningen, about every third inhabitant

---

[10] Cf. Maier 2004, p. 18.

[11] Kapff 1893: 10.

[12] Data: Hippel 1984, tabs 13, 54, 55; Württembergische Jahrbücher 1820 and following volumes; calculation by the author.

[13] Cf. Kirn 2017.

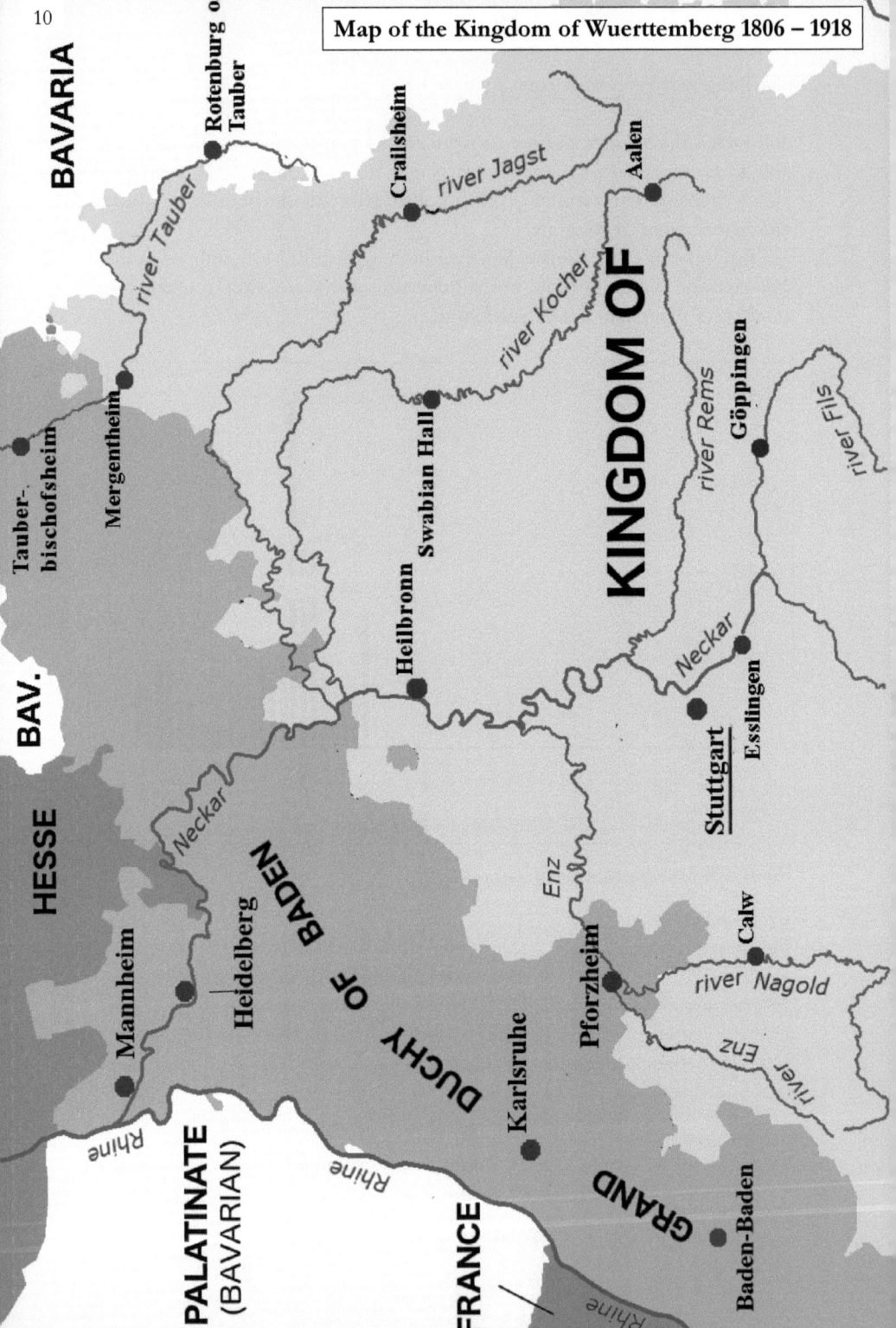

Map of the Kingdom of Wuerttemberg 1806 – 1918

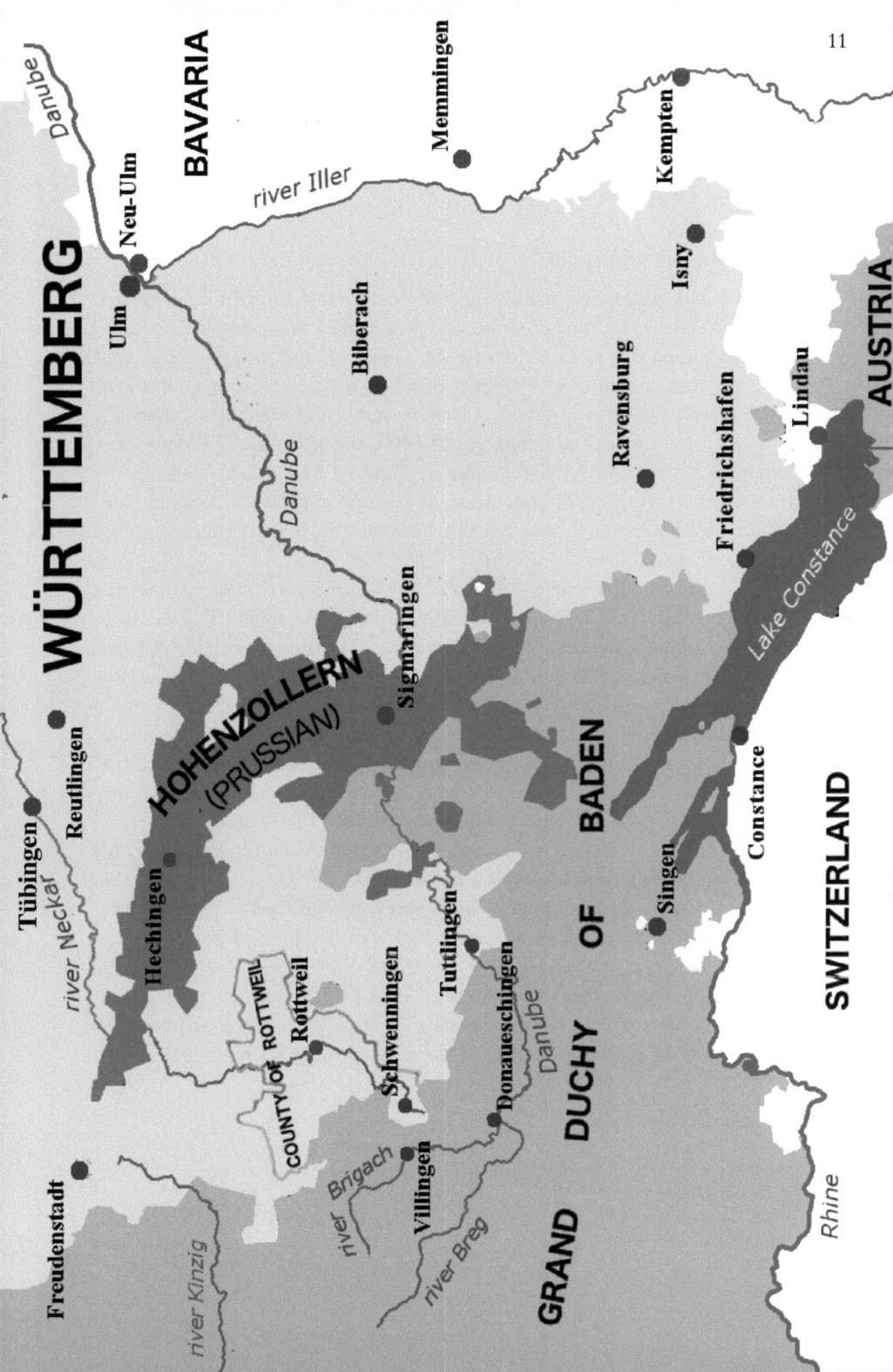

suffered from starvation. The population fed on grass and roots. Bread was made from tree bark and sawdust.[14]

Hunger again and again

The cause of hunger was mainly the bad weather that brought farming to a standstill. The agricultural crisis began when, after a long winter, the spring of 1816 turned out to be extremely dry. This was followed by a wet and cold summer, which even brought snowfall in July. Because of the low temperatures, 1816 went down in history as a "year without a summer". That year was the second coldest since 1400, and because of the low temperatures the year was called "eighteen hundred and frozen to death".[15] Bad weather prevailed in large areas of Europe and North America, but southwestern Germany was hit the hardest: "In Wuerttemberg it was particularly bad."[16]

The cause of the bad weather was the Indonesian volcano Tambora. When the volcano erupted in 1815, it hurled gigantic amounts of ash into the atmosphere. The ash spread all over the atmosphere and shielded the earth from solar radiation - the sun was not warming the earth's surface anymore.[17]

In the Kingdom of Wuerttemberg heavy crop failures where the result. The cold let the potatoes rot. Heavy thunderstorms and hail destroyed the fruit crop on the trees. Long-lasting rain made it impossible to bring in the hay. And at harvest time in the fall, snow covered the fields.[18] The cereal, potato and grape harvests had completely failed in the end.[19] Two-thirds of the livestock perished or had to be slaughtered.[20] A large part of the Swabians considered emigration as a way out and fled to the warmer southeastern Europe and southern Russia – an exodus which reminds of today's climate or war refugees.

About 5,500 Swabians went to Bessarabia at the Black Sea, the Crimea, and to the banks of the Volga. Another 2,500 Wuerttemberg refugees set off to a very long journey in 1816/1817 and set out to a lengthy journey to

---

[14] Cf. Hennings 2016.
[15] Volkmann 2016.
[16] Maier 2016, pp. 172/73.
[17] Cf. Maier 2016, p. 172.
[18] Cf. Hennings 2016.
[19] Cf. Maier 2016, p. 173.
[20] Cf. Ekbal 2006, pp. 3-4.

Tiflis, south of Caucasus Mountains near the border with the Ottoman Empire and Persia. This was about 2,500 miles from Wuerttemberg. The emigrants needed about one and a half years to arrive.[21] Many emigrants did not survive the journey. "The journey was marked by total disorder on and even before they reached Odessa, two-thirds of the emigrants had already died."[22] When they finally arrived at the destination, the survivors founded Swabian villages, built churches and began to grow wine, a knowledge they had brought with them from their home country Wuerttemberg. In the wine and cognac production, the Swabian colonies in the Caucasus region soon played an "exemplary role"[23].

While most other German emigrants left their homeland in 1816 and 1817 due to the volcanic eruption in Indonesia, many emigrated Swabians had additional religious motives: They were Pietists, christians who extremly focused on prayer and hard as well as joyless work. They had seen the volcanic eruption and also the previous wars of Napoleon, as the punishment of God. And they awaited the end of time, which, as they believed, should come on June 18, 1836. The Pietists planned to go to the Mount Ararat, as soon as the apocalypse and the second coming of Christ would have been imminent. The Ararat is located about 150 miles behind the Ottoman border. It was the mountain, where Noah's Ark had landed, a place of God. These emigrants also fled – like other Germans – from bad harvests and hunger, but the main driver for the journey in the Caucasus was the nearby Parousia.[24]

In the years 1831 and 1832, again, many Swabians left their homeland. As in the previous crisis, the population did not have enough food or could not pay for the food due to the repeatedly drastically increased prices.[25] Also during this phase of the crisis, some thousands of Pietists from Wuerttemberg moved to the southern slope of the Caucasus, as well as during the next emigration phase.[26]

This third phase of emigration began in 1845. It lasted until 1854 and then weakened. The reason for leaving Wuerttemberg were consistently below-average harvests throughout this decade. Food prices rose again,

---

[21] Cf. Ekbal 2006, pp. 10-11.

[22] Ekbal 2006, p. 12.

[23] Krieger 2016.

[24] Cf. Ekbal 2006, pp. 8-10; 13-14.

[25] Cf. Hippel 1948, p. 143.

[26] Cf. Ekbal 2006, p. 8.

and at the same time wages fell and population growth increased dramatically.[27] The lack of food reached its peak in 1846 and 1847, when particularly strong crop failures occured. As the hunger crisis continued in 1848, a wave of revolutions flared up throughout Europe.[28] When the Wuerttemberg revolution failed in 1849, not only did starving Swabians went abroad, but now also those parts of the population fled from Wuerttemberg that had engaged in the revolution.[29]

At the peak of emigration, in the three years from 1852 to 1854, 50,000 Swabians officially left their homeland. The number decreased in the 1860s, when Wuerttemberg's economic situation had improved noticeably.[30]

Swabian Emigration to North America

Although from the beginning of the 18th century, when the first Swabians emigrated to North America, this destination was initially rather a marginal phenomenon.[31]

Even if data series for the first decades of the 19th century are missing, individual years can be analyzed. Even though in the famine years of 1816 and 1817 some 20,000 Swabians fled abroad, not even 3 percent (546) of them embarked to North America. As far as can be seen, the number of

Year	%	Year	%	Year	%	Year	%
1815	0,7	1847	83,2	1855	72,8	1863	36,3
1816	14,8	1848	71,4	1856	72,3	1864	57,9
1817	0,6	1849	78,5	1857	77,7	1865	49,4
1822	1,6	1850	64,9	1858	60,2	1866	71,9
1827	4,4	1851	83,0	1859	57,2	1867	68,3
1832	6,7	1852	90,4	1860	63,1	1868	58,6
1837	3,7	1853	94,2	1861	65,1	1869	58,1
1842	5,1	1854	92,9	1862	41,4		

Tab.: Proportion of North American immigrants to all emigrants from Wuerttemberg 1815–1869.[32]

---

[27] Cf. Hippel 1984, pp. 180/81.
[28] Cf. Hippel 1984, pp. 142/43.
[29] Cf. Hippel 1984, p. 151.
[30] Cf. Hippel 1984, p. 174.
[31] Cf. Maier 2004a, p. 18.
[32] Data: Württembergisches Jahrbuch 1816 and following volumes.

Swabian emigrants, who reached North America, remained below 15 percent in the first decades of the 19th century. North America did not become an important emigrant destination until the mid-19th century (see figure p. 9), in particular until 1847, when the proportion of North American travelers abruptly increased to more than 80 percent of all Swabian refugees (see table p. 14).

Not until the agricultural crisis of the late 1840s, North America became the predominant immigration area of the Swabians. At the peak of this crisis, in the first half of the 1850s, almost all emigrants from Wuerttemberg (more than 90 percent) sailed across the Atlantic. As the bad weather phases stopped in the second half of the 1850s and the crops got better, the immigration to the US decreased again, too. The American Civil War reduced immigration numbers even further. However, in 1864/1865, the war prevented neither Johannes Würthner nor Maria Käfer from leaving Schwenningen for the US, though Johannes' brother's Martin and Baldus fought in the war.

All in all, between 1816 and 1871, officially around 400,000 people of the Kingdom of Wuerttemberg left for North America,[33] between 1871 and 1890 followed by another 100,000 Swabians.[34]

When Germans talked about North America, this phrase was mostly a synonym for the United States. The official statistics included under the heading North America, not only immigration into the US, but also into the northern located British colonies of later Canada. The extent of immigration of German or Swabian people can only roughly be estimated. "A precise calculation of Germans, who settled permanently in British North America is difficult to make."[35] Overall, only a small fraction of Swabian emigrants went to the British colonies. "Between 1851 und 1870 some 1,749,200 Germans immigrated to the United States while Canada received 52,400 new Germans."[36] Thus, only 3 percent of Germans left North America after Canada. The peak reached this emigration wave to Canada around 1851. Southwest Germany, where, once again, the peasants suffered particularly from crop failures and overpopulation, was anew especially affected.[37]

---

[33] Cf. Hippel 1984, p. 115.
[34] Cf. Württembergisches Jahrbuch 1892, p. 18.
[35] Wagner 2006, p. 25.
[36] Wagner 2006, p. 25.
[37] Cf. Wagner 2006, p. 249.

The Wuerttemberg authorities saw the emigration ambivalently. The emigration was not only at the initiative of the emigrants, but also the cities and communities started to encourage their population to leave. "The local authorities supported the emigration to master the impoverishment and to get rid of unwelcome poor residents." [38] Income-poor could count on state support for the costs of emigration. The municipalities thus tried to lower their social spending.[39] That's why the community Schwenningen paid 190 inhabitants in 1847 for emigrating to the United States.[40] The community lost around five percent of the 3,500 inhabitants at one stroke. Canada also benefited from such assistance. Baden, Hesse and Wuerttemberg dissolved entire rural communities "and shipped them to Québec and Saint John at public expense".[41] "Both Baden and Wuerttemberg dumped some of their poor in Canada."[42]

At the same time, the emigration was not free. The road to foreign countries led up above many bureaucratic hurdles. To leave Wuerttemberg, the emigrants had to pay their debts and wait for the exit permit. In addition to this official emigration, however, there was also an illegal escape from Wuerttemberg. The illegal emigration increased the population decline by 80 percent. Between 1843 and 1871 officially about 187,000 people left their kingdom. Another 150,000 people emigrated without logging out with the authorities.[43]

Matters of the heart as a motive of emigration

When Johannes Würthner and Maria Käfer emigrated to the US in the 1860s (to finally drag along Maria Käfer's mother and her other daughters and sons as well as some grandchildren), there were no crop failures in the Kingdom of Wuerttemberg any more. In the mid-1860s, agriculture and the economy recovered. After 1871, the year of founding of the German Reich, there was a big economic boom.[44] Presumably, the two also had no political and religious reasons.

---

[38] Hübner 2017.
[39] Cf. Kirn 2017.
[40] Cf. Brunner 2009, p. 59.
[41] Hübner 2017.
[42] Wagner 2006, p. 57.
[43] Cf. Hippel 1984, p. 139; own calculations.
[44] Cf. Kirn 2017.

The main reason for the emigration of Johannes Würthner and Maria Käfer might have been matters of the heart. This is suggested by the chronological sequences. As a start, Johannes Würthner went alone in July 1864 and without accompaniment to the United States. His future wife Maria Käfer followed him only a little while later. She reached New York in January or February 1865. (Exact date is missing.) And then it only took a few weeks up until February 22nd, and Johannes and Maria were married.

The subject "Marriage in the US" was common in the Kingdom of Wuerttemberg. For example, the Wuerttemberg illustrated entertainment weekly *Über Land und Meer* ("Over land und sea") published a story about the twosome Eugen and Emma. Those two also wanted to go to the US to marry. Eugen should travel ahead and prepare for the new life abroad. But that took a long time. "The years went by in their eventful run, and the two lovers remained separated. Over in America, Eugen struggled to build a solid existence for his bride."[45] And she was waiting for him. It took ten years, but then, Emma followed her financé to the US and they got married.[46]

Many couples wanted to marry in the US, because in many German states strict marriage laws existed. In the 18th century, it was already difficult to get the approval to marry. In Wuerttemberg had a ban on marriage, and the royal sovereign had to authorize the weddings. Usually, the approval for marrying was only given, if the newly-weds would leave Wuerttemberg immediately. Or the couples fled abroad to marry.[47] By limiting and controlling marriages, the Kingdom of Wuerttemberg and the communities wanted to ensure that couples had enough money to feed a family. The authorities did not want to be responsible for the upkeep of the newborn children.[48]

In 1807, the marriage restrictions were initially lifted under the influence of the French Revolution. Anyone who had a Wuerttemberg citizenship was now allowed to marry. Later the freedom to marry was limited again: From 1833, only those could get the citizenship, that were self-

---

[45] Wickede 1864, p. 396.
[46] Cf. Wickede 1864, p. 396.
[47] Cf. Scheuerbrandt 1985, p. 3.
[48] Cf. Müller 2003, p. 94.

employed and did not depend on poor support. This prevented poorer
Swabians from marrying.[49]

In 1852, a further tightening of the marriage conditions followed: Now
only the Swabian who had a financial fortune and regular income were
allowed to marry. 1852 to 1863 saw the period of the strictest marriage restrictions in the Kingdom of Wuerttemberg.[50] "Some couples, which were
affected by marriage restrictions, immigrated to North America to marry."[51] Especially couples from Wuerttemberg went to the US to marry.[52]
Though Johannes Würthner and Maria Käfer went only about a year after
the end of the strictest marriage restrictions to the US, their emigration
would still be influenced by these. Finally, on December 30, 1870, all still
existent marriage restrictions were lifted again.[53]

Chance or danger?

Those who leave their homeland must have the certainty that life in the
new home is that much better so it is worth the effort of emigration.[54]
While the emigrants hoped for a better life in the US, the Wuerttemberg
press usually drew a negative picture of the country.

Although the newspapers acknowledged that the United States had
given the world new civic perspectives. "The North-American Union ren-
dered outstandig services to both freedom and human dignity."[55] Or the
press praised the democratic rights, the "political equality"[56] and the "aware-
ness of self-government".[57]

But descriptions of a seducement to a bad way of life and dangers took
up most of the space. Therefore the weekly *Über Land und Meer* warned
against visions:

> *"With what golden dreams most of the emigrants go to America, as if
> they expect all the wonders of the land of milk and honey there - and
> how quickly these dreams melt into vain mist when the foot enters the*

---

[49] Cf. Müller 2003, p. 95.
[50] Cf. Müller 2003, p. 95.
[51] Krebber 2014, p. 210.
[52] Cf. Scheuerbrandt 1985, p. 3.
[53] Cf. Müller 2003, p. 95.
[54] Cf. Marschalck 1973, p. 17.
[55] Deutschland 1865, p. 824.
[56] C. M. 1867, p. 527.
[57] C. M. 1867, p. 527.

open ground of the land of longing! The roasted pigeons that fly in America's milk country, if you just bother opening your mouth, are nothing more than a funny children's tale.[58]

The reality would be less pleasant. German workers would be lured to faraway countries with the promise of a "carefree future" to "exploit them there and then abandon them to misery and destruction".[59] Many emigrants would fall among the thieves or frauds.[60] Others would die in the course. "The poor - only a few of them will find the hoped-for happiness over the ocean over there. Many, on the other hand, will perish in the storm of bloody civil war, which is already raging for four years."[61]

But death not only threatened because of the civil war, but also because of the American natives who sought immigrants for their lives. "The hair of some of these red-cheeked peasant boys, who are drawn to the forests of the far west, will end on the belt of an Indian as a booty."[62]

And not only the body, also the soul would be endangered in the US, for example at dance events. The daily *Schwäbische Kronik* („Swabian Cronicle") warned women explicitly of American amusement:

"Don't you find yourself, after you have danced, feasted your eyes, joked, eaten and drunk, the next day dissatisfied and deceived? What influence does this inadequately spent night have on you? The answer: a sick head stunned by the music, a barren heart filled with impure images, tired limbs, unfit for work or Sunday worship, a burdened conscience, and an enlarged list of sins."[63]

Reports came from America, the daily *Schwäbische Kronik* wrote, that women went to hell because of dancing – "Big, ghastly, underground vaults, in it every 10 paces, a big fire",[64] where "wailing of many souls"[65] can be heard.

While the press drew a distorted negative image, those willing to emigrate were generally better and more credibly informed. Many emigrants wrote letters to the old homeland, in which they described a much more

---

[58] Farmers Frühstücksruhe, Des, 1868, p. 814.
[59] Telegramm 1865, p. 1115.
[60] Cf. Menzel 1864, p. 249.
[61] Wickede 1864a, p. 787.
[62] Estván 1864, p. 148.
[63] Wort an Ball-Besuchende, Ein, 1864, p. 204.
[64] Wort an Ball-Besuchende, Ein, 1864, p. 205.
[65] Wort an Ball-Besuchende, Ein, 1864, p. 205.

positive reality. "Such correspondences were very often the origin of the emigration of other individuals or families from a particular place or area."[66] In this way, also Johannes Würthner's brother Jakob - who had gone to the US in June 1848 - would have sent letters to the family in Schwenningen, which could have strengthened the desire for emigration.

Literatur

C. M. (1867): "New Yorker Skizzen, 1. Knickerbocker." *Über Land und Meer* No. 33/May, pp. 527-530.

"Deutschland" (1865): *Schwäbischer Merkur*, May 11, p. 824.

Ekbal, K. (2006): "Die deutsche Auswanderung 1816/1817 in den Kaukasus und ihre millenaristischen Hintergründe." *Beiträge des 'Irfán-Kolloqiums*, vol. 3: 1-17, bahai-library.com/pdf/e/ekbal_deutsche_auswanderung.pdf (10.1.2018).

Estvàn, B. (1864): "Eine Reise nach dem amerikanischen Kriegsschauplatze." *Über Land und Meer* No. 10/December, pp. 148-150.

"Farmers Frühstücksruhe, Des" (1868). *Über Land und Meer* No. 51/*September*, p. 814.

Fertig, G. (2000): "Familienrekonstitutionsmethode und Analyse sozialer Ungleichheit: Ein oberrheinisches Beispiel." *Geschichtliche Landeskunde*, issue 50, pp. 81-89, www.regionalgeschichte.net/bibliothek/texte/aufsaetze/fertig-familienrekonstitutionsmethode.html (12.12.2017).

Fies, A. (2010): "Die badische Auswanderung im 19. Jahrhundert nach Nordamerika unter besonderer Berücksichtigung des Amtsbezirks Karlsruhe zwischen 1880–1914." Karlsruhe: KIT Scientic Publishing, www.google.de /url?sa=t&rct=j&q=&esrc=s&source=web&cd=18&cad=rja&uact=8&ve d=0ahUKEwil7Y22-afYAhXKKewKHTQ7B9Y4ChAWCEgwBw&url= https%3A%2F%2Fwww.ksp.kit.edu%2Fdownload%2F1000012905&usg= AOvVaw3-is1YdUNvMZP9PS4YEr3p (10.1.2018).

Güll, R. (2013): "Auswanderung aus Württemberg und Baden." *Statistisches Monatsheft Baden-Württemberg* , issue 9, pp. 41-48, www.statistik-bw.de/ Service/Veroeff/Monatshefte/PDF/Beitrag13_09_08.pdf (15.12.2017).

---

[66] Scheuerbrandt 1985, p. 4.

Hennings, Andreas (2016): "Die Hungersnot von 1816/17." *Schwarzwälder Bote* online, April 7th, www.schwarzwaelder-bote.de/inhalt.villingen-schwennin gen-die-hungersnot-von-1816-17.69de5070-50d2-45a7-9ab8-a15c2b6a 4903.html (30.10.2017).

Hippel, W. von (1984): "Auswanderung aus Südwestdeutschland. Studien zur württembergischen Auswanderung und Auswanderungspolitik im 18. und 19. Jahrhundert." Stuttgart: Klett Cotta.

Hochstuhl, K. (2017): "Die Auswanderung nach Übersee. Auf der Suche nach wirtschaftlichem Auskommen und politischer Freiheit." Landeskunde Baden-Württemberg online. edited by Landeszentrale für politische Bildung Baden-Württemberg, www.landeskunde-baden-wuerttemberg.de/ auswanderung_uebersee.html (30.10.2017).

Hübner, H.-J. (2017): "Deutsche in Kanada." Version 1.224, March 22, www.geschichte-kanadas.de/Canada_ethnic/_deutsche.html, 2017 (10.1.2018).

Kapff, P. (1893): "Schwaben in Amerika seit der Entdeckung des Weltteils." *Württembergische Neujahrsblätter*, issue 10.

Kirn, D. (2017): "Auswanderung." Landeskunde Baden-Württemberg online, edited by Landeszentrale für politische Bildung Baden-Württemberg, http://www.landeskunde-baden-wuerttemberg.de/auswanderung.html (30.10.2017).

Krebber, J. (2014): "Württemberger in Nordamerika. Migration von der Schwäbischen Alb im 19. Jahrhundert." Stuttgart: Franz Steiner Verlag.

Klutes, A. (1991): "Die Seeschiffe des Norddeutschen Lloyd." Vol. 1: 1857 – 1919. Herford: Köhlers.

Krieger, V. (2016): "250 Jahre in Russland, in der UdSSR und in den Ländern der GUS." Portal Landeskunde Baden-Württemberg, edited by Landeszentrale für politische Bildung Baden-Württemberg, www.landeskunde-baden-wuerttemberg.de/russlanddeutsche_hintergrund.html#c33536 (16.12.2017).

Lienert, E. M./W. Lienert (2004): "Neue Heimat in Amerika – Massenauswanderung im 19. Jahrhundert." *Deutschland und Europa*, Issue 45: Migration, edition 3, pp. 23-25, www.deutschlandundeuropa.de/45_02/ Migration.pdf (1.11.2017).

Maier, U. (2004a): "Auswanderung nach Nordamerika im 18. und 19. Jahrhundert." *Deutschland und Europa*, Issue 45: Migration, edition 3, pp. 18-20, www.deutschlandundeuropa.de/45_02/Migration.pdf (1.11.2017).

Maier, U. (2004b): "Schwabenzüge – die Auswanderung nach Russland, Polen und die Donauländer." *Deutschland und Europa*, Issue 45: Migration, edition 3, pp. 11-12.

Maier, U. (2005): "Migration als Thema der Landesgeschichte." Landesgeschichte in Forschung und Unterricht, issue 1, pp. 9-23.

Maier, U. (2016): "'Die Armut treibt mich fort.' Massenauswanderung aus der Heilbronner Region in die Vereinigten Staaten von Amerika im 18. und zu Beginn des 19. Jahrhunderts." Heilbronnica, Beiträge zur Stadt- und Regionalgeschichte, vol. 6, pp. 169-212.

[Menzel, W.] (1864): "Reisen." *Wolfgang Menzels Literaturblatt* No. 63/August 6, pp. 249-252.

Müller, R. (2003): "Heiratsalter und Ehehindernisse in Stuttgart-Feuerbach im 19. und frühen 20. Jahrhundert." Historical Social Research 28, 3, pp. 92-109, www.ssoar.info/ssoar/bitstream/handle/document/5062/ssoar-hsr-2003-no_3__no_105-muller-heiratsalter_und_ehehindernisse_in_stuttgart-feuerbach.pdf?sequence=1 (10.1.2018).

Neubaur, P. A. F. (1907): "Der norddeutsche Lloyd. 50 Jahre der Entwicklung. 1857-1907." Vol. 1, Leipzig: Verlag von Friedrich Wilhelm Grunow, ia802702.us.archive.org/31/items/bub_gb_SncvAAAAYAAJ/bub_gb_SncvAAAAYAAJ.pdf (18.1.2018).

Scheuerbrandt, A. (1985): "Die Auswanderung aus dem heutigen Baden-Württemberg." *Historischer Atlas von Baden-Württemberg*, issue 10, No. 12,5, edited by Kommission für Geschichtliche Landeskunde in Baden-Württemberg, www.leo-bw.de/media/kgl_atlas/current/delivered/pdf/HABW_12_5.pdf (12.12.2017).

"Telegramm" (1865). In: *Schwäbischer Merkur*, October 18, p. 1115.

Volkmann, I. (2016): "Das Jahr ohne Sommer 1816. Massenexodus aus dem Armenhaus." *Stuttgarter Zeitung* online, July 27, www.stuttgarter-zeitung.de/inhalt.das-jahr-ohne-sommer-1816-massenexodus-aus-dem-armenhaus.0771767e-12c5-43a4-bae1-749473685cfb.html (18.1.2018).

Wagner, J. (2006): "A History of Migration from Germany to Canada, 1850-1939." Vancouver/Toronto: UBC Press.

Wickede, J. von (1864a): "Ein Besuch der österreichischen Kriegsflotte auf der Rhede bei Cuxhafen." *Über Land und Meer* No. 9/September, pp. 787-790.

Wickede, J. von (1864b): "Bilder aus dem schleswig-holsteinischem Kriege von 1848–50." *Über Land und Meer* No. 25/March, pp. 395-396.

"Wort an Ball-Besuchende, Ein" (1864): *Schwäbische Kronik*, January 28, pp. 204-205.

Genealogical Tree of the Family Branch Johannes Würthner/Maria Käfer

Stefan Matysiak

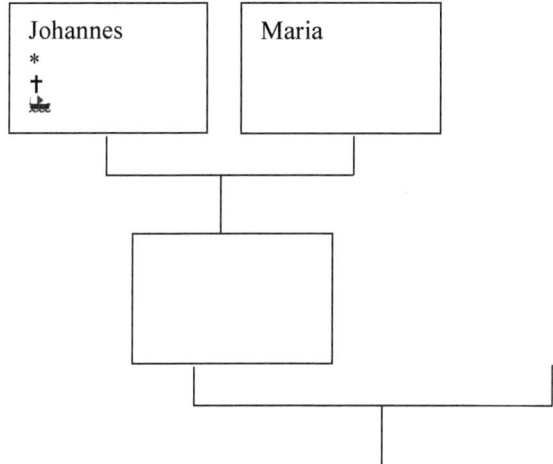

Legend: * day of birth   † death   marriage   ⚓ immigration
1912 census (US federal and New York state)

Date format: DD-MM-YYYY

Data: Angela Matysiak, Beate Adomeit, Stefan Matysiak

Würthner

Jakob
* 08.02.1789 in Schwenningen
† 11.12.1850 in Schwenningen
⚭ 28.10.1817 in Schwenningen

Schlenker

Katharina
* 20.09.1797 in Schwenningen
† 25.02.1871 in Schwenningen

Würthner

Johannes (John Wirtner)
* 20.03.1843 in Schwenningen
† 14.08.1894 in Buffalo, NY
18.07.1864; Ship name: „America", Departure harbour: Bremen
1880 Watchmaker
1892 Machinist
⚭ 22.2.1865

Wirtner, John Jacob
* 4.9.1866 in Buffalo, NY
† 22.8.1935, San Francisco, CA
1880 Clerk in Store

Wirtner, Albert Martin
* 24.12.1867 in Buffalo
† 16.07.1956
1880 Cigar Maker
01.07.1920
⚭ **Day**, Katherine
* about 1878

Wirtner, Mary
* 02.05.1869 in Buffalo
† 02.11.1950 in Buffalo
1880 At School
1892 Tailoress
before 1910
⚭ **Leydecker**, George F.
* about 1871

Wirtner, Erhard
* 22.06.1870 in Buffalo
† 18.07.1870 in Buffalo

Wirtner, Richard
* 02.08.1871 in Buffalo
† 21.12.1873 in Buffalo

Käfer

Martin

* 27.01.1812 in Schwenningen
† 20.04.1861 in Schwenningen
⚭ 21.06.1837 in Schwenningen

Mauthe

Agnes (Agnes Catherine Mauthé)

* 06.06.1816 (or 16.06.1816)
† 18.11.1882 (Hamilton, Buttler, O.
1905 Head of family
⚰ 31.07.1868 in New York

Also to the USA: her children Agnes
(*1835), Anna (*1836), Agathe
Vösseler born Käfer (*1837), Martin
(* 1850), Christina (*1852), Ursula
(*1853), Johannes (*1856), Rosina
(*1858), and Christian (*1859) as well
as the granddaughters Anna (*1859)
and Maria Vösseler (*1861).

Käfer

Maria (Mary Wirtner)

* 11.10.1843 in Schwenningen
† 31.10.1909 in Hamilton, OH
⚰ 1865

Wirtner, Christina Agnes

* 13.03.1873 in Buffalo
1880 At School
1892 Tailoress
1905 Dressmaker, living with her
mother Mary and siblings

Wirtner, Richard

* 13.01.1875 in Buffalo
March 1963 in New York
1880 At School
1892 Machinist
1905 Machinist
1910 Living in Buffalo, with his
sister Mary A. Leydecker
born Wirtner

Wirtner, Catharina

* 16.01.1877 in Buffalo
† 20.04.1877 in Buffalo

Wirtner, Rosa (Rose)

* 20.09.1878 in Buffalo
1905 Dressmaker
1910 Living in Buffalo, with her
sister Mary A. Leydecker

Wirtner, Laura Mathilda

* 15.04.1883 in Buffalo

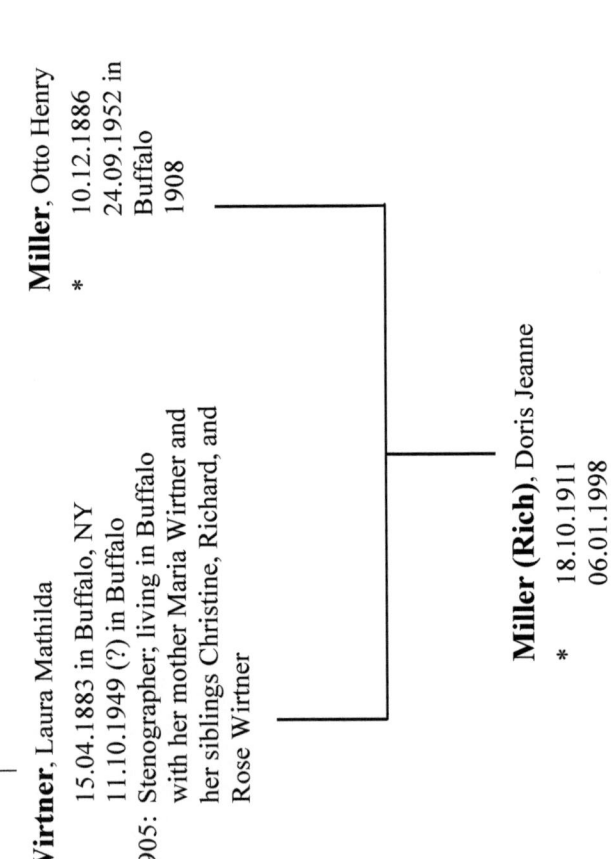

Miller, Otto Henry

*   10.12.1886
     24.09.1952 in
     Buffalo
     1908

Wirtner, Laura Mathilda

*   15.04.1883 in Buffalo, NY
     11.10.1949 (?) in Buffalo
1905: Stenographer; living in Buffalo
     with her mother Maria Wirtner and
     her siblings Christine, Richard, and
     Rose Wirtner

Miller (Rich), Doris Jeanne

*   18.10.1911
     06.01.1998

Schwenningen Family Tree,
Genealogical Tables

Beate Adomeit

NN

Anna
* um 1611
† 08.08.1697 Schwenningen

Genealogical table no. 1

Subsequent table

Würthner
Jakob
* 01.01.1732 Schwenningen
† 08.03.1797 Schwenningen
⚭ 09.05.1753 Schwenningen
> 2

Benzing
Anna
* 18.11.1730 Schwenningen
† 19.09.1767 Schwenningen
> 3

Würthner
Jakob
* 02.02.1742 Schwenningen
† 07.02.1812 Schwenningen
⚭ 11.11.1767 Schwenningen
> 4

Kaiser
Barbara
* 20.01.1747 Schwenningen
† 18.12.1807 Schwenningen
> 5

Schlenker
Johannes
* 19.09.1733 Schwenningen
† 19.11.1802 Schwenningen
⚭ 04.02.1756 Schwenningen
> 6

Schlenker
Katharina
* 15.06.1734 Schwenningen
† 28.02.1812 Schwenningen
> 7

Hanßmann
Martin
* in Tuningen
⚭
> 8

Rapp
Anna
* 25.08.1731 Schwenningen
† 05.03.1792 Schwenningen

Würthner
Martin
* 17.09.1764 Schwenningen
† 24.02.1856 Schwenningen
⚭ 15.04.1788 Schwenningen

Würthner
Katharina
* 03.03.1769 Schwenningen
† 21.04.1819 Schwenningen

Schlenker
Balthes
* 20.08.1767 Schwenningen
† 17.06.1835 Schwenningen
⚭ 14.07.1789 Schwenningen

Hanßmann
Anna Maria
* 09.10.1767 von Tuningen
† 07.09.1848 Schwenningen

Würthner
Jakob
* 08.02.1789 Schwenningen
† 11.12.1850 Schwenningen
⚭ 28.10.1817 Schwenningen

Schlenker
Katharina
* 20.09.1797 Schwenningen
† 25.02.1871 Schwenningen

Würthner
Johannes, Watchmaker (1880)
* 20.03.1843 Schwenningen
† 14.08.1894 Ausgwandert
⚭ um 1864 ?

Wirtner
Laura Mathilda, Stenographer (1905)
* 15.04.1883

Käfer
Maria
* 11.10.1843 Schwenningen
† Amerika

Käfer
Martin
* 27.01.1812 Schwenningen
† 20.04.186? Schwenningen
⚭ 21.06.1837 Schwenningen

Mauthe
Agnes
* 06.06.1816 Schwenningen
† Amerika

Käfer
Martin
* 12.10.1784 Schwenningen
† 20.03.1841 Schwenningen
⚭ 29.01.1811 Schwenningen

Müller
Anna
* 26.09.1791 Schwenningen
† 07.03.1840 Schwenningen

Mauthe
Johann Georg
* 06.10.1781 Schwenningen
† 20.07.1845 Schwenningen
⚭ 27.02.1810 Schwenningen

Mauthe
Agnes
* 01.03.1789 Schwenningen
† 27.04.1848 Schwenningen

Käfer
Martin
* 21.01.1757 Schwenningen
† 20.03.1841 Schwenningen
⚭ 24.09.1782 Schwenningen
> 9

Maier
Ursula
* 27.01.1763 Schwenningen
† 02.04.1837 Schwenningen
> 10

Müller
Martin
* 02.05.1756 Schwenningen
† 20.02.1812 Schwenningen
⚭ 11.06.1782 Schwenningen
> 11

Jauch
Katharina
* 20.11.1757 Schwenningen
† 29.10.1815 Schwenningen
> 12

Mauthe
Jakob
* 15.01.1749 Schwenningen
† 12.08.1825 Schwenningen
⚭ 14.02.1775 Schwenningen
> 13

Kayser
Maria
* 23.02.1755 Schwenningen
† 24.08.1816 Schwenningen
> 14

Mauthe
Caspar
* 09.09.1763 Schwenningen
† 27.05.1802 Schwenningen
⚭ 27.07.1786 Schwenningen
> 15

Jäckle
Agnes
* 22.11.1762 Schwenningen
> 16

Genealogical table no. 2

Würthner
Erhard
* um 1612 Schwenningen
† 20.09.1694 Schwenningen
∞

Schneider
Margaretha
* um 1619 Fluon
† 06.10.1689 Schwenningen

Schuler
Ludwig
* um 1621 Schwenningen
† 17.02.1686 Schwenningen
∞

NN
Anna
* um 1611
† 08.08.1697 Schwenningen

Schmidt
Hans
* um 1610 von Erzingen
∞

Weber
Valentin
* um 1601
† 22.01.1686 Schwenningen
∞

NN
Maria
* um 1609
06.04.1687 Schwenningen

Würthner
Jakob
* um 1645 Schwenningen
† 25.03.1690 Schwenningen
∞ 02.11.1669 Schwenningen

Schuler
Catharina
* um 1653 Schwenningen
† 15.02.1726 Schwenningen

Schmidt
Konrad
* um 1642 Schwenningen
† 13.11.1682 Schwenningen
∞ 24.01.1671 Schwenningen

Weber
Anna Katharina
* 22.01.1652 Schwenningen
† 15.05.1736 Schwenningen

Würthner
Jakob
* 19.09.1677 Schwenningen
† 08.04.1740 Schwenningen
∞ 24.01.1702 Schwenningen

Schmidt
Catharina
* 15.12.1689 Schwenningen
† 16.01.1756 Schwenningen

Würthner
Balthas
* 15.12.1702 Schwenningen
† 17.04.1776 Schwenningen
∞ 19.10.1723 Schwenningen

von Tafel 1
Würthner
Jakob
* 01.01.1732 Schwenningen
† 08.03.1797 Schwenningen
∞ 09.05.1753 Schwenningen

Hauser
Michael
* um 1616 Schwenningen
† 25.04.1693 Schwenningen
⚭ vor 1639 Schwenningen

Krebs
Anna
* um 1617 vom Brigachtal
† 24.04.1679 Schwenningen

Boper
Hans
* um 1620 in Otefingen
⚭

Schuler
Ludwig
* um 1621 Schwenningen
† 17.02.1686 Schwenningen
⚭ 2)

Link
Anna
* um 1611 Schwenningen
† 08.08.1697 Schwenningen

Benzing
Christian
* um 1620 Schwenningen
† 16.03.1715 Schwenningen
⚭ um 1649 Schwenningen

Kienzle
Anna
* um 1630
† 08.06.1686 Schwenningen

Hauser
Matthiss
* vor 1639 Schwenningen
† 09.07.1707 Schwenningen
⚭ 18.10.1671 Schwenningen

Boppin
Regula
* um 1647 von Otefingen
† 07.01.1687 Schwenningen

Schuler
Ludwig
* um 1647 Schwenningen
† 28.11.1714 Schwenningen
⚭ 30.04.1673 Schwenningen

Benzing
Agathe
* 07.02.1653 Schwenningen
† 05.01.1718 Schwenningen

Hauser
Johannes(Hanß)
* 24.06.1683 Schwenningen
† 01.06.1714 Schwenningen
⚭ 17.10.1701 Schwenningen

Schuler
Anna
* 28.07.1681 Schwenningen
† 02.02.1720 Schwenningen

Hauser
Anna
* 29.08.1706 Schwenningen
† 05.12.1775 Schwenningen

Benzing
Anna
* 18.11.1730 Schwenningen
† 19.09.1767 Schwenningen

Genealogical table no. 3

Benzing
Christian
* um 1620 Schwenningen
† 16.03.1715 Schwenningen
∞ um 1649 Schwenningen
Kienzle
Anna
* um 1630
† 08.06.1686 Schwenningen

Reiser
Jakob
* 31.03.1623 Talheim
† 12.04.1713
∞ um 1646 Talheim
Irion
Ursula
* 27.04.1618 Talheim
† 27.08.1703

Benzing
Johannes(Hanß)
* 02.02.1655 Schwenningen
† 14.02.1716 Schwenningen
∞ 21.11.1675 Schwenningen

Reiser
Ursula
* um 1649 Talheim
† 12.06.1716 Schwenningen

Messner
Martin
* 1654 Trossingen
† 03.03.1730 Trossingen
∞ 2) 06.06.1676 Trossingen

Kohler
Anna
* Trossingen
† vor 00.10.1686 Trossingen

Benzing
Christian
* 18.09.1680 Schwenningen
† 01.06.1752 Schwenningen
∞ 07.06.1701 Schwenningen

Messner
Katharina
* 23.03.1677 Trossingen
† 30.06.1755 Schwenningen

Benzing
Hans Martin
* 17.02.1704 Schwenningen
† 01.10.1776 Schwenningen
∞ 08.02.1724 Schwenningen

von Tafel 1
Benzing
Anna
* 18.11.1730 Schwenningen
† 19.09.1767 Schwenningen
∞ 09.05.1753 Schwenningen

Würthner
Jakob
* 01.01.1732 Schwenningen
† 08.03.1797 Schwenningen

Link
Anna
* 22.03.1707 Schwenningen
† 28.09.1772 Schwenningen

Link
Andreas
* 02.03.1681 Schwenningen
† 25.07.1757 Schwenningen
⚭ 20.10.1705 Schwenningen

Biedermann
Maria
* 08.10.1685 Schwenningen
† 01.02.1754 Schwenningen

Link
Jakob
* 05.09.1641 von Schura
† 30.01.1690 Schwenningen
⚭ 2)   31.01.1665 Schwenningen

Benzing
Anna
* um 1639 Schwenningen
† 01.09.1719 Schwenningen

Biedermann
Jakob
* 06.01.1660 Schwenningen
† 09.01.1720 Schwenningen
⚭ 23.06.1686 Schwenningen

Irion
Maria
* um 1647 Schwenningen
† 31.01.1724 Schwenningen

Benzing
Jakob
* 1604 Schwenningen
† 1679 Schwenningen
⚭ 2)   vor 1639

NN
Maria
* um 1606 Schwenningen
† 27.02.1681 Schwenningen

Biedermann
Hannß
* um 1621 Schwenningen
† 13.01.1684 Schwenningen
⚭ 1639 Schwenningen

Ottlins
Salome
* um 1625 aus der Schweiz

Irion
Hans Heinrich
* um 1616 in Talheim
† 24.05.1691 Schwenningen
⚭

Haps
Maria
* 01.05.1613 von Talheim ?
† 22.10.1691 Schwenningen

Genealogical table no. 4

Würthner
Erhard
* um 1612 Schwenningen
† 20.09.1694 Schwenningen
⚭

Schneider
Margaretha
* um 1619 Fluon
† 06.10.1689 Schwenningen

Schuler
Ludwig
* um 1621 Schwenningen
† 17.02.1686 Schwenningen
⚭

NN
Anna
* um 1611
† 08.08.1697 Schwenningen

Schmidt
Hans
* um 1610 von Erzingen
⚭

Weber
Valentin
* um 1601
† 22.01.1686 Schwenningen
⚭

NN
Maria
* um 1609
† 06.04.1687 Schwenningen

Würthner
Jakob
* um 1645 Schwenningen
† 25.03.1690 Schwenningen
⚭ 02.11.1669 Schwenningen

Schuler
Catharina
* um 1653 Schwenningen
† 15.02.1726 Schwenningen

Schmidt
Konrad
* um 1642 Schwenningen
† 13.11.1682 Schwenningen
⚭ 24.01.1671 Schwenningen

Weber
Anna Katharina
* 22.01.1652 Schwenningen
† 15.05.1736 Schwenningen

Würthner
Jakob
* 19.09.1677 Schwenningen
† 08.04.1740 Schwenningen
⚭ 24.01.1702 Schwenningen

Schmidt
Catharina
* 15.12.1689 Schwenningen
† 16.01.1756 Schwenningen

Würthner
Erhard
* 15.01.1708 Schwenningen
† 21.07.1782 Schwenningen
⚭ 13.08.1737 Schwenningen

von Tafel 1
Würthner
Jakob
* 02.02.1742 Schwenningen
† 07.02.1812 Schwenningen
⚭ 11.11.1767 Schwenningen

Schlenker
Jakob
* 1611 Schwenningen
† 28.05.1688 Schwenningen
⚭ um 1643 Schwenningen

Lauffer
Agatha
* um 1622 Schwenningen
† 25.02.1690 Schwenningen

Schrenk
Hanß
* um 1630 Schwenningen
† 06.04.1676 Schwenningen
⚭ um 1653 Schwenningen

Müller
Agathe
* um 1623 Schwenningen
† 01.09.1701 Schwenningen

> 17

Lauffer
Jacob
* um 1622 Schwenningen
† 25.09.1674 Schwenningen
⚭ 16.06.1663 Schwenningen

> 18

Kaiser
Anna
* um 1647 Schwenningen
† 25.12.1671 Schwenningen

> 19

Schuler
Ludwig
* um 1647 Schwenningen
† 28.11.1714 Schwenningen
⚭ 30.04.1673 Schwenningen

> 20

Benzing
Agathe
* 07.02.1653 Schwenningen
† 05.01.1718 Schwenningen

Schlenker
Bartholomäus
* 15.07.1660 Schwenningen
† 06.08.1735 Schwenningen
⚭ 16.02.1683 Schwenningen

Schrenk
Barbara
* 09.04.1662 Schwenningen
† 20.10.1740 Schwenningen

Lauffer
Georg
* 09.12.1668 Schwenningen
† 06.12.1742 Schwenningen
⚭ 1694 Schwenningen

Schuler
Maria
* 25.02.1674 Schwenningen
† 18.11.1715 Schwenningen

Schlenker
Martin
* 26.10.1689 Schwenningen
† 29.09.1741 Schwenningen
⚭ 18.06.1715 Schwenningen

Lauffer
Agathe
* 29.01.1685 Schwenningen
† 25.04.1767 Schwenningen

Schlenker
Maria
* 26.04.1716 Schwenningen
† 13.10.1795 Schwenningen

Kaiser
Barbara
* 20.01.1747 Schwenningen
† 18.12.1807 Schwenningen

Genealogical table no. 5

> 21

Kaiser
Jakob
* um 1617 Schwenningen
† 01.12.1688 Schwenningen
∞ 5)
NN
Anna

Benzing
Jakob
* 1604 Schwenningen
† 1679 Schwenningen
∞ 2) vor 1639
NN
Maria
* um 1606 Schwenningen
† 27.02.1681 Schwenningen

Lauffer
Christian
* um 1618 Schwenningen
† 22.09.1678 Schwenningen
∞ 24.01.1651 Schwenningen
Schlenker
Anna
* um 1615 Schwenningen
† 25.03.1675 Schwenningen

Würthner
Jakob
* um 1645 Schwenningen
† 25.03.1690 Schwenningen
∞ 2) 02.11.1669 Schwenningen
Schuler
Katharina
* 1653

Kaiser
Gabriel
* um 1648 Schwenningen
† 08.12.1692 Schwenningen
∞ 22.10.1671 Schwenningen

Benzing
Katharina
* um 1646 Schwenningen
† 18.12.1714 Schwenningen

Lauffer
Georg
* 05.05.1668 Schwenningen
† 26.08.1743 Schwenningen
∞ 12.02.1689 Schwenningen

Würthner
Anna
* 14.10.1670 Schwenningen
† 26.03.1736 Schwenningen

Kaiser
Jakob
* 14.06.1671 Schwenningen
† 12.08.1756 Schwenningen
∞ 08.05.1714 Schwenningen

Lauffer
Katharina
* 18.07.1696 Schwenningen
† 21.02.1764 Schwenningen

Kaiser
Georg
* 22.08.1716 Schwenningen
† 24.04.1760 Schwenningen
∞ 19.11.1744 Schwenningen

von Tafel 1
Kaiser
Barbara
* 20.01.1747 Schwenningen
† 18.12.1807 Schwenningen
∞ 11.11.1767 Schwenningen

Würthner
Jakob
* 02.02.1742 Schwenningen
† 07.02.1812 Schwenningen

Schlenker
Katharina
* 04.04.1722 Schwenningen
† 23.04.1753 Schwenningen

Schlenker
Erhard
* 21.11.1679 Schwenningen
† 24.12.1757 Schwenningen
⚭ 28.04.1711 Schwenningen

Schlenker
Christian
* um 1640 Schwenningen
† 18.05.1711 Schwenningen
⚭ 09.02.1664 Schwenningen

Schlenker
Christian
* um 1615 Schwenningen
† 26.02.1663 Schwenningen
⚭ 1638 Schwenningen

Mäder
Elisabetha
* um 1615 Schlachten bei Schaffhausen

Rosenfelder
Barbara
* um 1641 Mönchweiler
† 12.03.1693 Schwenningen

Rosenfelder
Hanß
* Mönchweiler
⚭

Weyler
Barbara
* 24.11.1691 Schwenningen
† 14.03.1759 Schwenningen

Weyler
Georg
* 19.03.1662 Schwenningen
† 26.03.1743 Schwenningen
⚭ 15.06.1686 Schwenningen

Weyler
Georg
* um 1607 Schwenningen
† 21.12.1688 Schwenningen
⚭ 13.10.1656 Schwenningen

Hardter
Margaretha
* um 1634 Schwenningen
† 06.02.1679 Schwenningen

Schlenker
Barbara
* 25.07.1667 Schwenningen
† 15.04.1715 Schwenningen

Schlenker
Hanß
* um 1609 Schwenningen
† 01.08.1691 Schwenningen
⚭ 05.08.1666 Schwenningen

Schlenker
Barbara
* 1610 Schwenningen
† 01.05.1680 Schwenningen

Genealogical table no. 6

Schlenker
Erhard
* um 1605 Schwenningen
† 17.02.1678 Schwenningen
⚭ vor 1623 Schwenningen

Münch
Brigitta
* um 1605
† 00.01.1653 Schwenningen

Müller
Vältin
* um 1603 Schwenningen
† 16.02.1673 Schwenningen
⚭ vor 1651 Schwenningen

Schlenker
Anna
* um 1607 Schwenningen
† 29.07.1679 Schwenningen

Schlenker
Joseph
* um 1623 Schwenningen
† 17.12.1665 Schwenningen
⚭ um 1653 Schwenningen

Müller
Barbara
* um 1627 Schwenningen
† 13.10.1671 Schwenningen

Haller
Jakob
* um 1615 Schwenningen
† 17.09.1698 Schwenningen
⚭ 2) um 1640 Schwenningen

Lauffer
Anna
* um 1620 Schwenningen
† um 1675 Schwenningen

Schlenker
Valentin
* 02.02.1660 Schwenningen
† 04.02.1722 Schwenningen
⚭ 09.05.1682 Schwenningen

Haller
Walburga
* 23.03.1655 Schwenningen
† 02.03.1731 Schwenningen

Schlenker
Johannes
* 09.01.1693 Schwenningen
† 27.03.1755 Schwenningen
⚭ 30.04.1720 Schwenningen

von Tafel 1
Schlenker
Johannes
* 19.09.1733 Schwenningen
† 19.11.1802 Schwenningen
⚭ 04.02.1756 Schwenningen

Schlenker
Katharina
* 15.06.1734 Schwenningen
† 28.02.1812 Schwenningen

Würthner
Katharina
* 10.07.1698 Schwenningen
† 30.10.1741 Schwenningen

Würthner
Erhard
* 17.10.1673 Schwenningen
† 13.11.1739 Schwenningen
⚭ 15.06.1697 Schwenningen

Würthner
Jakob
* um 1645 Schwenningen
† 25.03.1690 Schwenningen
⚭ 02.11.1669 Schwenningen

Würthner
Erhard
* um 1612 Schwenningen
† 20.09.1694 Schwenningen
⚭

Schneider
Margaretha
* um 1619 Fluon
† 06.10.1689 Schwenningen

Schuler
Catharina
* um 1653 Schwenningen
† 15.02.1726 Schwenningen

Schuler
Ludwig
* um 1621 Schwenningen
† 17.02.1686 Schwenningen
⚭

NN
Anna
* um 1611
† 08.08.1697 Schwenningen

Irion
Anna
* 17.13.1674 Öfingen
† 21.03.1746 Schwenningen

Irion
Johann
* um 1655 Tuningen
† 20.08.1725 Tuningen
⚭ 17.11.1674 Tuningen

Wölflin
Agnes
* 09.05.1654 in Öfingen
† 25.08.1725 Tuningen

Genealogical table no. 7

Schlenker
Christian
* um 1615 Schwenningen
† 26.02.1663 Schwenningen
⚭ 1638 Schwenningen

Mäder
Elisabetha
* um 1615 Schlachten bei Schaffhausen

Möst
Georg
* um 1610 Schwenningen
⚭

Laminithin
Anna
* um 1612 Schwenningen
† 26.12.1652 Schwenningen

Müller
Vältin
* um 1603 Schwenningen
† 16.02.1673 Schwenningen
⚭ 2)   um 1623 Schwenningen

Schlenker
Anna
* um 1607 Schwenningen
† 29.07.1679 Schwenningen

Schneckenburger
Bartl
* in Tuttlingen
⚭

Schlenker
Hans Martin
* um 1639 Schwenningen
† 02.01.1676 Schwenningen
⚭ 10.11.1663 Schwenningen

Möst
Barbara
* um 1638 Schwenningen
† 16.05.1724 Schwenningen

Müller
Balthas
* um 1621 Schwenningen
† 05.09.1707 Schwenningen
⚭ 14.05.1661 Schwenningen

Schneckenburger
Magdalena
* um 1635 Tuttlingen

Schlenker
Christian
* 16.08.1668 Schwenningen
† 29.03.1732 Schwenningen
⚭ 26.04.1692 Schwenningen

Müller
Agathe
* 01.06.1673 Schwenningen
† 17.05.1737 Schwenningen

Schlenker
Balthes
* 13.06.1700 Schwenningen
† 1762 Schwenningen
⚭ 26.10.1728 Schwenningen

von Tafel 1
Schlenker
Katharina
* 15.06.1734 Schwenningen
† 28.02.1812 Schwenningen
⚭ 04.02.1756 Schwenningen

> 22

> 23

Lauffer
Jacob
* um 1622 Schwenningen
† 25.09.1674 Schwenningen
⚭ 16.06.1663 Schwenningen

Kaiser
Anna
* um 1647 Schwenningen
† 25.12.1671 Schwenningen

Palmtag
Christian
* um 1628 Schwenningen
† 08.03.1719 Schwenningen
⚭ 21.06.1656 Schwenningen

Schlenker
Anna
* um 1639 Schwenningen
† 18.01.1723 Schwenningen

Biedermann
Hannß
* um 1621 Schwenningen
† 13.01.1684 Schwenningen
⚭ 1639 Schwenningen

Ottlins
Salome
* um 1625 aus der Schweiz

Irion
Hans Heinrich
* um 1616 in Talheim
† 24.05.1691 Schwenningen
⚭

Haps
Maria
* 01.05.1613 von Talheim ?
† 22.10.1691 Schwenningen

Lauffer
Christian
* 30.03.1664 Schwenningen
† 17.03.1744 Schwenningen
⚭ 02.10.1683 Schwenningen

Palmtag
Anna Maria
* 22.02.1664 Schwenningen
† 16.12.1729 Schwenningen

Biedermann
Jakob
* 06.01.1660 Schwenningen
† 09.01.1720 Schwenningen
⚭ 23.06.1686 Schwenningen

Irion
Maria
* um 1647 Schwenningen
† 31.01.1724 Schwenningen

Lauffer
Joh. Jakob
* 18.07.1684 Schwenningen
† 03.12.1758 Schwenningen
⚭ 18.11.1704 Schwenningen

Biedermann
Maria
* 08.10.1686 Schwenningen
† 01.02.1754 Schwenningen

Lauffer
Anna Maria
* 05.07.1706

Schlenker
Johannes
* 19.09.1733 Schwenningen
† 19.11.1802 Schwenningen

Genealogical table no. 8

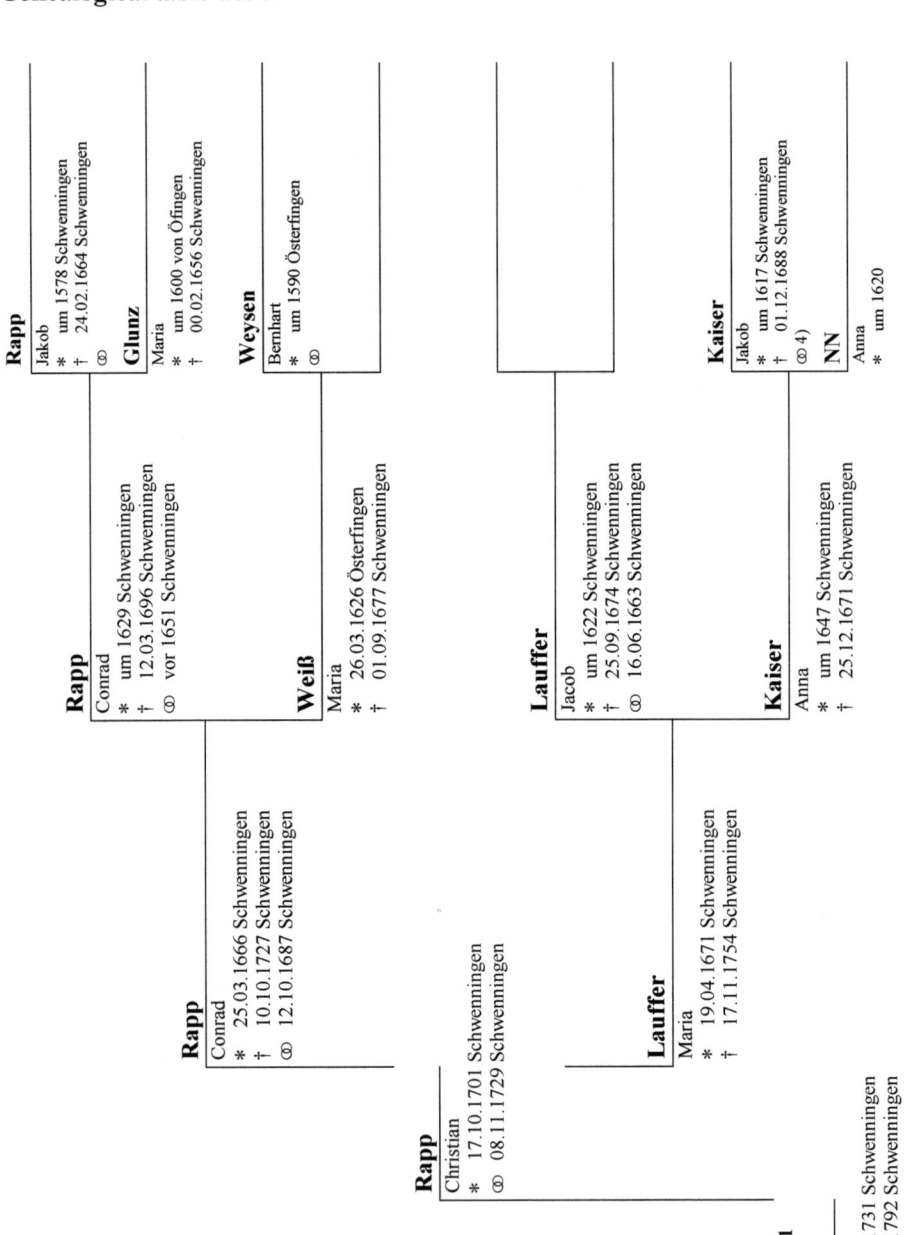

Rapp
Jakob
* um 1578 Schwenningen
† 24.02.1664 Schwenningen
∞

Glunz
Maria
* um 1600 von Öfingen
† 00.02.1656 Schwenningen

Weysen
Bernhart
* um 1590 Österfingen
∞

Kaiser
Jakob
* um 1617 Schwenningen
† 01.12.1688 Schwenningen
∞ 4)

NN
Anna
* um 1620

Rapp
Conrad
* um 1629 Schwenningen
† 12.03.1696 Schwenningen
∞ vor 1651 Schwenningen

Weiß
Maria
* 26.03.1626 Österfingen
† 01.09.1677 Schwenningen

Lauffer
Jacob
* um 1622 Schwenningen
† 25.09.1674 Schwenningen
∞ 16.06.1663 Schwenningen

Kaiser
Anna
* um 1647 Schwenningen
† 25.12.1671 Schwenningen

Rapp
Conrad
* 25.03.1666 Schwenningen
† 10.10.1727 Schwenningen
∞ 12.10.1687 Schwenningen

Lauffer
Maria
* 19.04.1671 Schwenningen
† 17.11.1754 Schwenningen

Rapp
Christian
* 17.10.1701 Schwenningen
∞ 08.11.1729 Schwenningen

von Tafel 1
Rapp
Anna
* 25.08.1731 Schwenningen
† 05.03.1792 Schwenningen
∞

Hanßmann
Martin
* in Tuningen

Schlenker
Agnes
* 24.10.1706 Schwenningen
† 19.04.1755 Schwenningen

Schlenker
Christianus
* 21.09.1555 Schwenningen
† 09.06.1723 Schwenningen
∞ 13.06.1582 Schwenningen

Schlenker
Hans
* um 1618 Schwenningen
† 17.02.1686 Schwenningen
∞ um 1647 Schwenningen

Schlenker
Erhard
* 1595 Schwenningen
† 1630 Schwenningen
∞

Benzing
Agatha
* um 1600 Schwenningen
† 1632 Schwenningen

Fuckher
Maria
* um 1627 Winterdingen ?
† 12.11.1693 Schwenningen

Fuckher
Conrad
* um 1600 Winterdingen Hohenstophlen
∞

Kremm
Anna
* um 1662 Talheim
† 09.01.1729 Schwenningen

Kremm
Hanß Martin
* Talheim
∞

Genealogical table no. 9

> 24

Käfer
Hans Jakob
* um 1622 Schwenningen
† 01.04.1671 Schwenningen
∞

Hauser
Brigitta
* um 1624 Schwenningen
† 10.08.1694 Schwenningen

Schlenker
Hanß
* um 1640 Schwenningen
† 08.11.1671 Schwenningen
∞

NN
Barbara

Jauch
Martin
* um 1637 Schwenningen
† 24.12.1678 Schwenningen
∞ 26.09.1671 Schwenningen

Irion
Maria
* um 1647 Schwenningen
† 31.01.1724 Schwenningen

Kämpf
Matthias
* in Oberbaldingen
∞

Käfer
Hans Conrad
* 05.07.1668 Schwenningen
† 21.07.1722 Schwenningen
∞ 05.05.1691 Schwenningen

Schlenker
Agathe
* 29.01.1671 Schwenningen
† 04.06.1703 Schwenningen

Jauch
Jakob
* 27.04.1677 Schwenningen
† 14.06.1726 Schwenningen
∞ 2) 02.11.1697 Schwenningen

Kämpf
Anna Katharina
* um 1668 von Oberbaldingen
† 09.01.1737 Schwenningen

Käfer
Conrad
* 26.03.1698 Schwenningen
† 05.03.1758 Schwenningen
∞ 29.01.1726 Schwenningen

Jauch
Maria
* 13.11.1698 Schwenningen
† 26.09.1750 Schwenningen

Käfer
Martin
* 19.10.1728 Schwenningen
† nach 09.03.1786 Schwenningen
∞ 27.11.1753 Schwenningen

von Tafel 1
Käfer
Martin
* 21.01.1757 Schwenningen
† 20.03.1841 Schwenningen
∞ 24.09.1782 Schwenningen

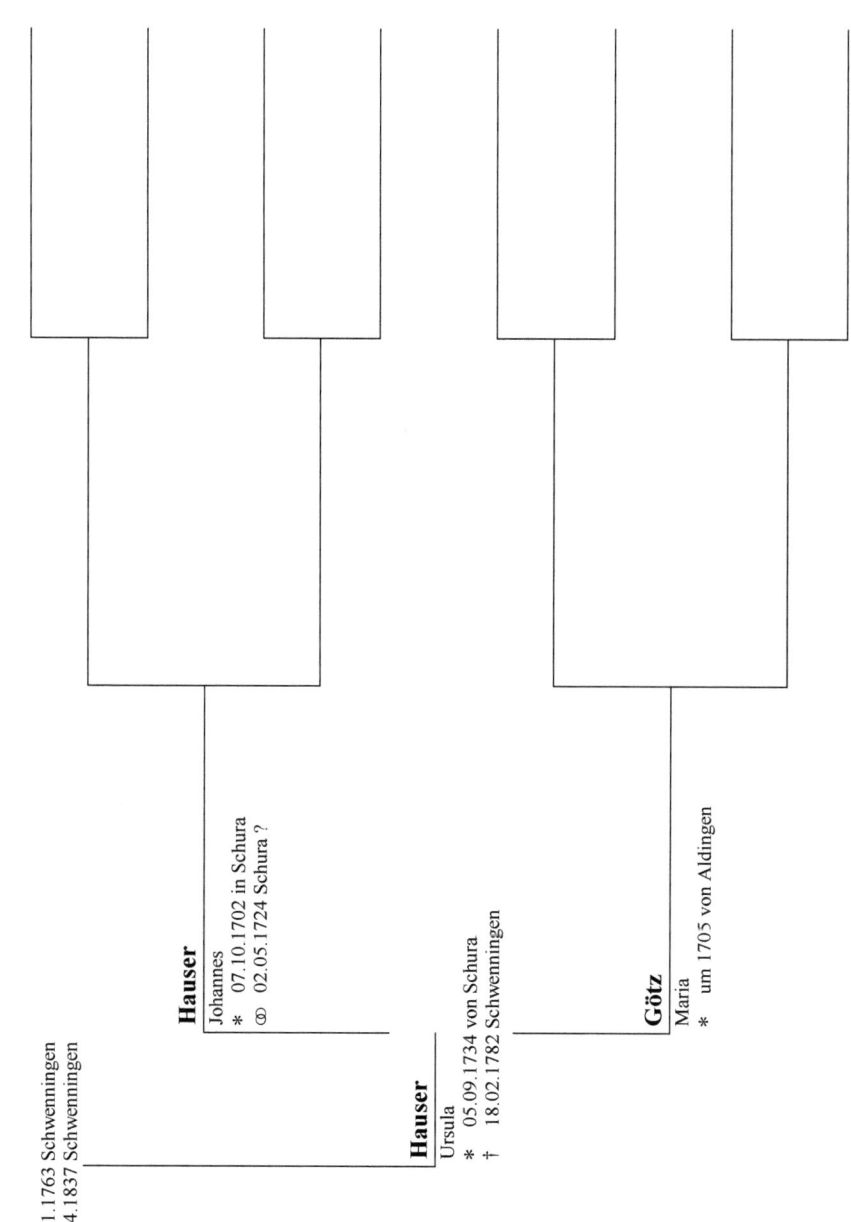

Maier
Ursula
* 27.01.1763 Schwenningen
† 02.04.1837 Schwenningen

Hauser
Johannes
* 07.10.1702 in Schura
⚭ 02.05.1724 Schura ?

Hauser
Ursula
* 05.09.1734 von Schura
† 18.02.1782 Schwenningen

Götz
Maria
* um 1705 von Aldingen

Genealogical table no. 10

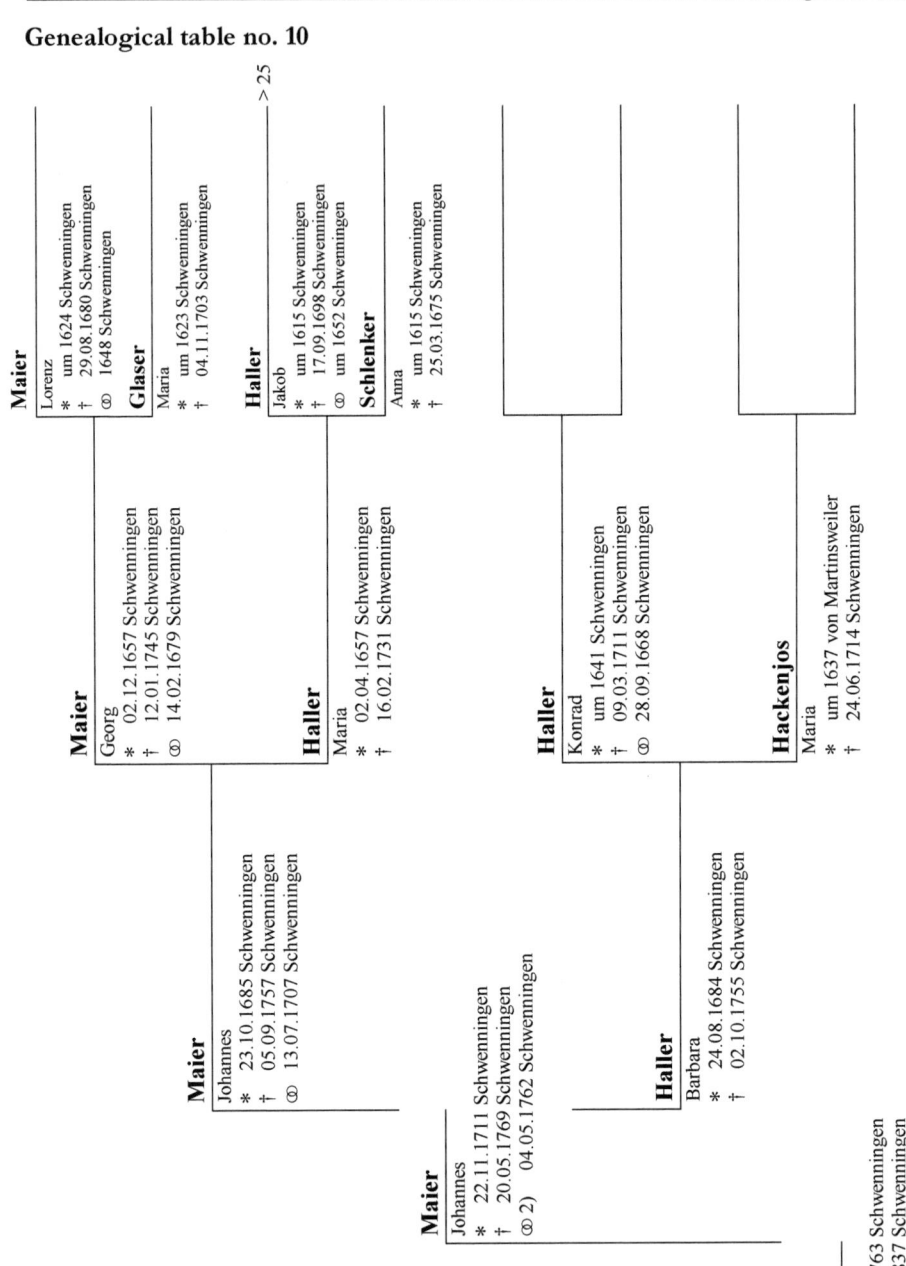

> 25

Maier
Lorenz
* um 1624 Schwenningen
† 29.08.1680 Schwenningen
⚭ 1648 Schwenningen

Glaser
Maria
* um 1623 Schwenningen
† 04.11.1703 Schwenningen

Haller
Jakob
* um 1615 Schwenningen
† 17.09.1698 Schwenningen
⚭ um 1652 Schwenningen

Schlenker
Anna
* um 1615 Schwenningen
† 25.03.1675 Schwenningen

Maier
Georg
* 02.12.1657 Schwenningen
† 12.01.1745 Schwenningen
⚭ 14.02.1679 Schwenningen

Haller
Maria
* 02.04.1657 Schwenningen
† 16.02.1731 Schwenningen

Haller
Konrad
* um 1641 Schwenningen
† 09.03.1711 Schwenningen
⚭ 28.09.1668 Schwenningen

Hackenjos
Maria
* um 1637 von Martinsweiler
† 24.06.1714 Schwenningen

Maier
Johannes
* 23.10.1685 Schwenningen
† 05.09.1757 Schwenningen
⚭ 13.07.1707 Schwenningen

Haller
Barbara
* 24.08.1684 Schwenningen
† 02.10.1755 Schwenningen

Maier
Johannes
* 22.11.1711 Schwenningen
† 20.05.1769 Schwenningen
⚭ 2) 04.05.1762 Schwenningen

von Tafel 1
Maier
Ursula
* 27.01.1763 Schwenningen
† 02.04.1837 Schwenningen
⚭ 24.09.1782 Schwenningen

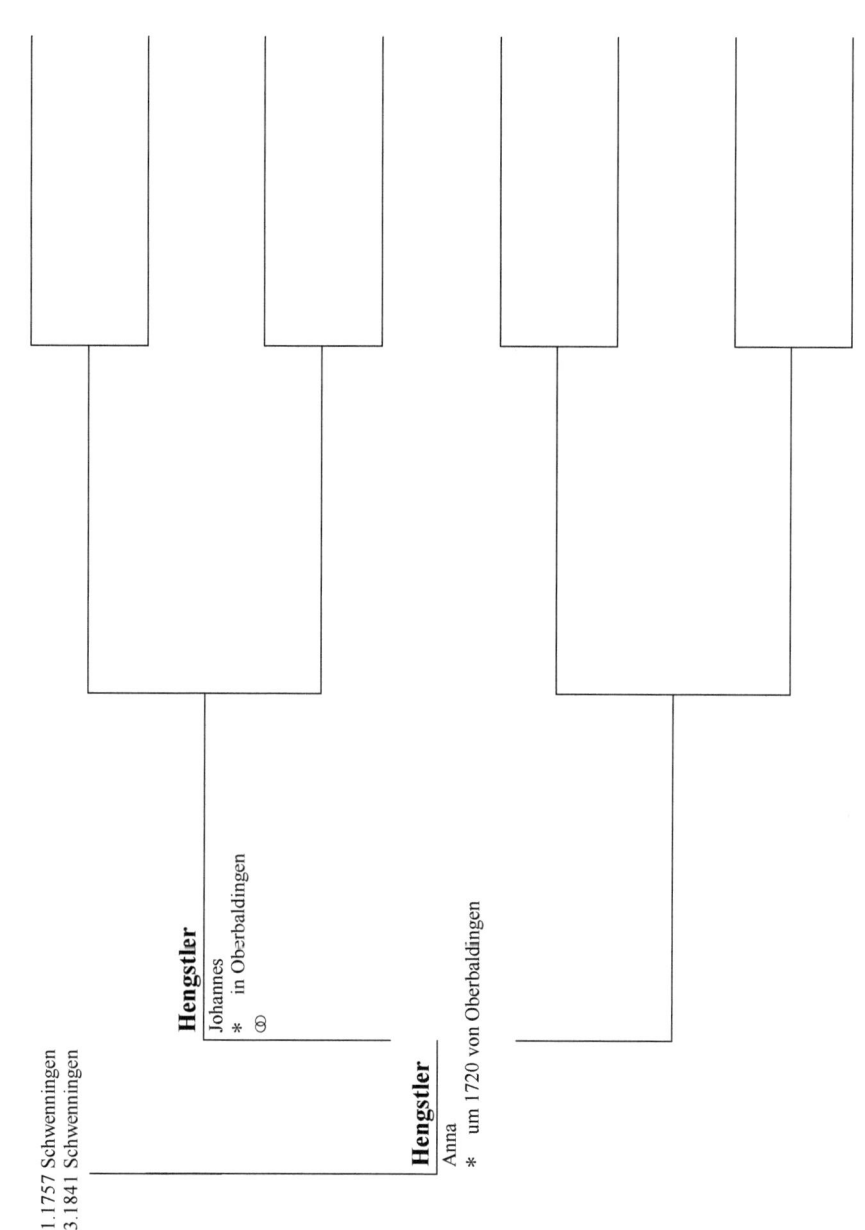

Käfer
Martin
* 21.01.1757 Schwenningen
† 20.03.1841 Schwenningen

Hengstler
Johannes
* in Oberbaldingen
∞

Hengstler
Anna
* um 1720 von Oberbaldingen

Genealogical table no. 11

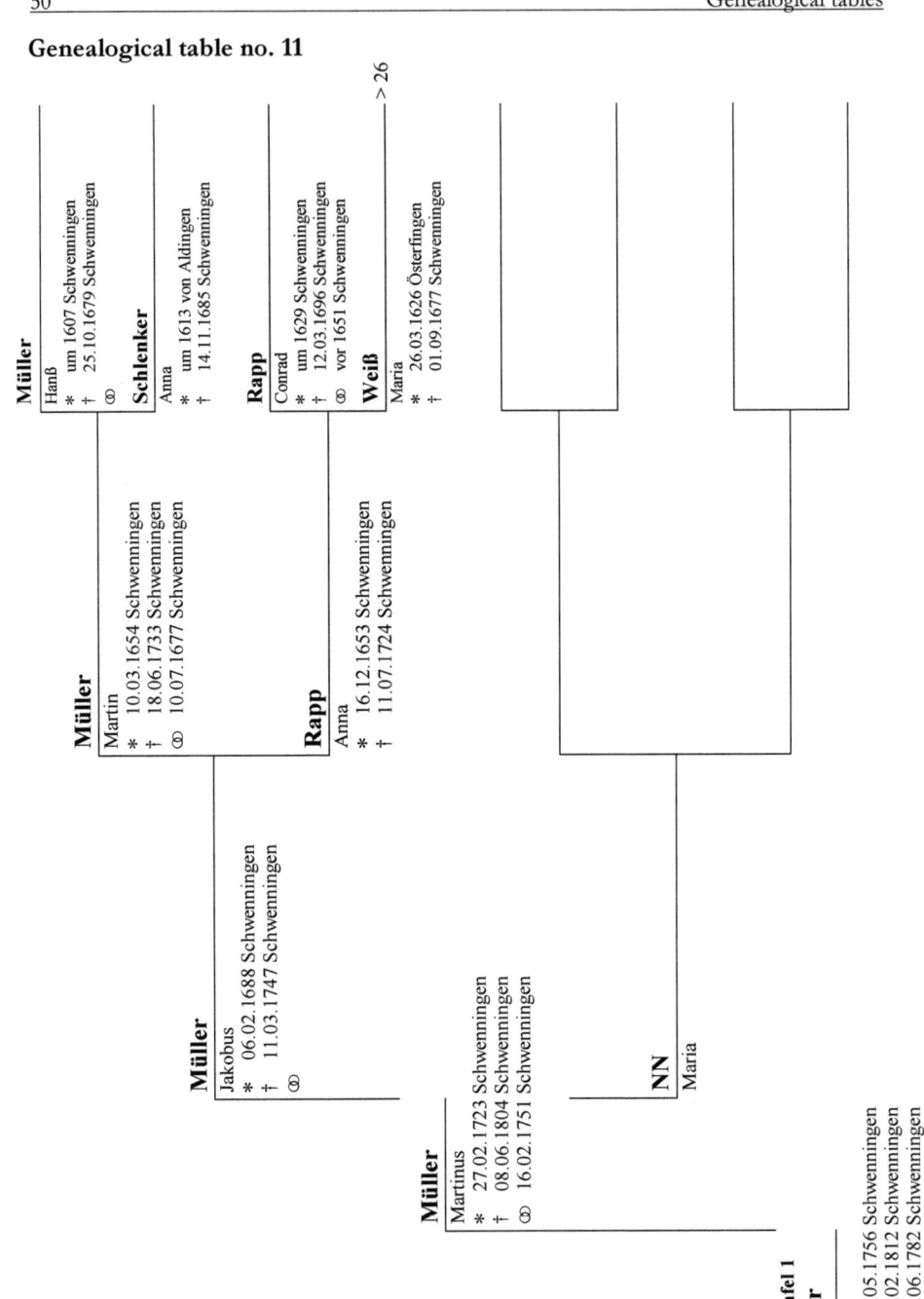

Müller
Hanß
* um 1607 Schwenningen
† 25.10.1679 Schwenningen
∞

Schlenker
Anna
* um 1613 von Aldingen
† 14.11.1685 Schwenningen

Rapp
Conrad
* um 1629 Schwenningen
† 12.03.1696 Schwenningen
∞ vor 1651 Schwenningen

Weiß
Maria
* 26.03.1626 Österfingen
† 01.09.1677 Schwenningen

> 26

Müller
Martin
* 10.03.1654 Schwenningen
† 18.06.1733 Schwenningen
∞ 10.07.1677 Schwenningen

Rapp
Anna
* 16.12.1653 Schwenningen
† 11.07.1724 Schwenningen

Müller
Jakobus
* 06.02.1688 Schwenningen
† 11.03.1747 Schwenningen
∞

NN
Maria

Müller
Martinus
* 27.02.1723 Schwenningen
† 08.06.1804 Schwenningen
∞ 16.02.1751 Schwenningen

von Tafel 1
Müller
Martin
* 02.05.1756 Schwenningen
† 20.02.1812 Schwenningen
∞ 11.06.1782 Schwenningen

> 27

Kaiser
Jakob
* um 1617 Schwenningen
† 01.12.1688 Schwenningen
⚭ 5)
NN
Anna

Benzing
Jakob
* 1604 Schwenningen
† 1679 Schwenningen
⚭ 2)　vor 1639
NN
Maria
* um 1606 Schwenningen
† 27.02.1681 Schwenningen

Lauffer
Christian
* um 1618 Schwenningen
† 22.09.1678 Schwenningen
⚭ 24.01.1651 Schwenningen

Schlenker
Anna
* um 1615 Schwenningen
† 25.03.1675 Schwenningen

Würthner
Jakob
* um 1645 Schwenningen
† 25.03.1690 Schwenningen
⚭ 2)　02.11.1669 Schwenningen

Schuler
Katharina
* 1653

Kaiser
Gabriel
* um 1648 Schwenningen
† 08.12.1692 Schwenningen
⚭ 22.10.1671 Schwenningen

Benzing
Katharina
* um 1646 Schwenningen
† 18.12.1714 Schwenningen

Lauffer
Georg
* 05.05.1668 Schwenningen
† 26.08.1743 Schwenningen
⚭ 12.02.1689 Schwenningen

Würthner
Anna
* 14.10.1670 Schwenningen
† 26.03.1736 Schwenningen

Kaiser
Jakob
* 14.06.1691 Schwenningen
† 12.08.1756 Schwenningen
⚭ 08.05.1714 Schwenningen

Lauffer
Katharina
* 18.07.1696 Schwenningen
† 21.02.1764 Schwenningen

Kaiser
Anna
* 14.07.1730 Schwenningen

Jauch
Katharina
* 20.11.1757 Schwenningen
† 29.10.1815 Schwenningen

Genealogical table no. 12

> 28

Jauch
Michael
* um 1621 Schwenningen
† 30.03.1693 Schwenningen
⚭ 1639

Jauch
Katharina
* um 1611 Schwenningen
† 12.03.1663 Schwenningen

Kohler
Jakob
* 25.08.1635 in Talheim
† 23.02.1721 Talheim
⚭

Schneckenburger
Anna
* 00.04.1634 Talheim
† 24.10.1699 Talheim

Müller
Hanß
* um 1607 Schwenningen
† 25.10.1679 Schwenningen
⚭

Schlenker
Anna
* um 1613 von Aldingen
† 14.11.1685 Schwenningen

Rapp
Conrad
* um 1629 Schwenningen
† 12.03.1696 Schwenningen
⚭ vor 1651 Schwenningen

Weiß
Maria
* 26.03.1626 Österfingen
† 01.09.1677 Schwenningen

Jauch
Hanß
* 19.08.1655 Schwenningen
† 16.01.1733 Schwenningen
⚭ 03.03.1685 Schwenningen

Kohler
Catharina
* 13.02.1664 Talheim
† 04.04.1714 Schwenningen

Müller
Martin
* 10.03.1654 Schwenningen
† 18.06.1733 Schwenningen
⚭ 10.07.1677 Schwenningen

Rapp
Anna
* 16.12.1653 Schwenningen
† 11.07.1724 Schwenningen

Jauch
Jakob
* 26.02.1686 Schwenningen
† 20.07.1774 Schwenningen
⚭ 14.02.1713 Schwenningen

Müller
Katharina
* 12.03.1693 Schwenningen
† 10.01.1758 Schwenningen

Jauch
Martin
* 11.11.1725 Schwenningen
† 01.02.1798 Schwenningen
⚭ 04.05.1751 Schwenningen

von Tafel 1
Jauch
Katharina
* 20.11.1757 Schwenningen
† 29.10.1815 Schwenningen
⚭ 11.06.1782 Schwenningen

> 29

> 30

Müller
Martin
* 02.05.1756 Schwenningen
† 20.02.1812 Schwenningen

Link
Martin
* 20.07.1699 Schwenningen
† 20.11.1775 Schwenningen
⚭ 02.11.1729 Schwenningen

Link
Maria
* 09.02.1728 Schwenningen
† 23.09.1774 Schwenningen

Link
Martin
* 12.11.1665 Schwenningen
† 24.01.1714 Schwenningen
⚭ 06.08.1690 Schwenningen

Schuler
Anna
* 07.10.1670 Schwenningen
† 29.01.1735 Schwenningen

Kreutter
Christina
* um 1699 von Talheim
† 12.12.1753 Schwenningen

Link
Jakob
* 05.09.1641 von Schura
† 30.01.1690 Schwenningen
⚭ 2) 31.01.1665 Schwenningen

Benzing
Anna
* um 1639 Schwenningen
† 01.09.1719 Schwenningen

Schuler
Hanß
* um 1646 Schwenningen
† 22.09.1692 Schwenningen
⚭ 30.04.1667 Schwenningen

Lauffer
Anna
* um 1646 Schwenningen
† 01.04.1687 Schwenningen

Kreutter
Ulrich
* in Talheim
⚭

Genealogical table no. 13

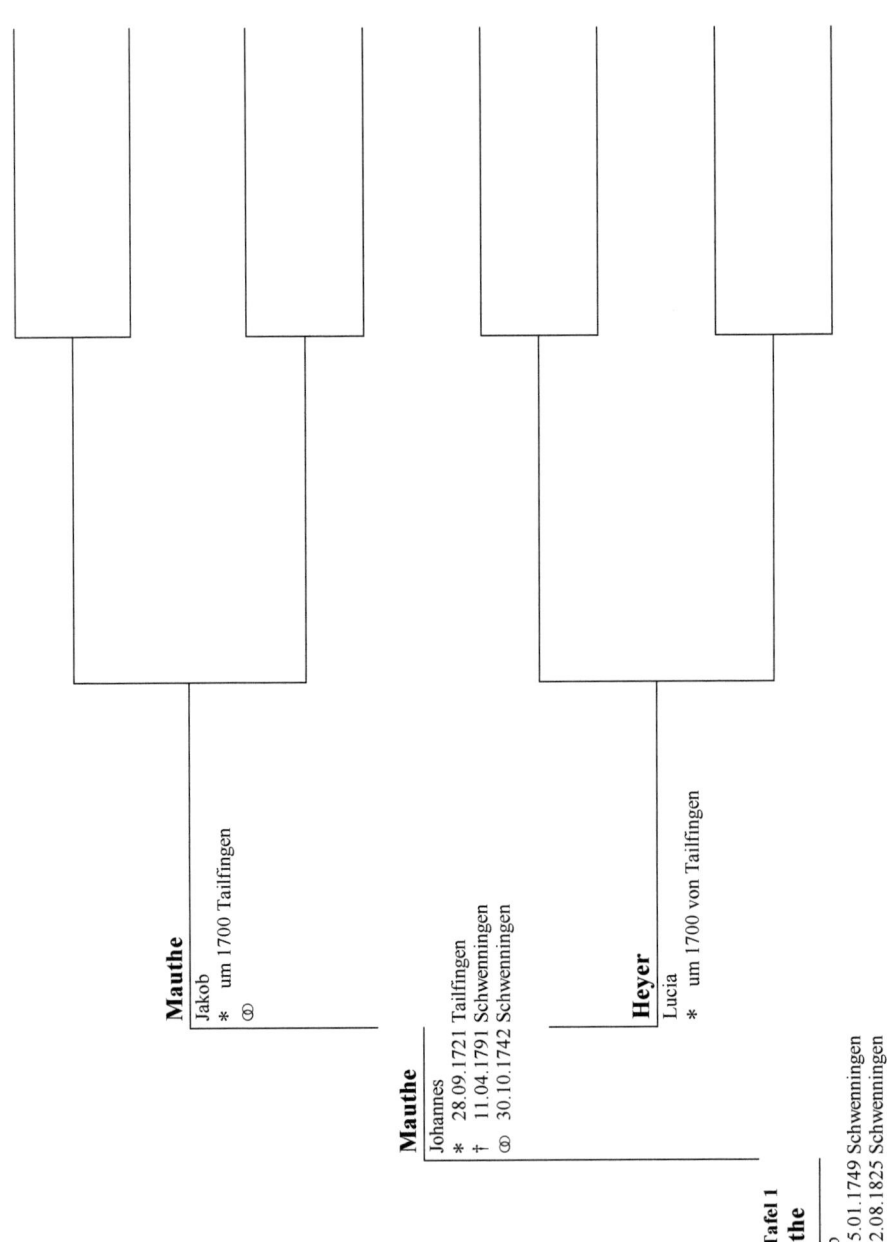

Mauthe
Jakob
* um 1700 Tailfingen
⚭

Mauthe
Johannes
* 28.09.1721 Tailfingen
† 11.04.1791 Schwenningen
⚭ 30.10.1742 Schwenningen

Heyer
Lucia
* um 1700 von Tailfingen

von Tafel 1
Mauthe
Jakob
* 15.01.1749 Schwenningen
† 12.08.1825 Schwenningen
⚭ 14.02.1775 Schwenningen

Kayser
Maria
* 23.02.1755 Schwenningen
† 24.08.1816 Schwenningen

Maier
Christina
* 12.03.1721 Schwenningen
† 20.09.1796 Schwenningen

Maier
Christian
* 04.12.1685 Schwenningen
† 22.11.1761 Schwenningen
⚭ 28.06.1718 Schwenningen

Lauffer
Agnes
* 06.01.-696 Schwenningen

Maier
Johannes
* 05.10.1654 Schwenningen
† 04.10.1724 Schwenningen
⚭ 04.06.1676 Schwenningen

Lauffer
Agathe
* 03.12.1654 Schwenningen
† 19.02.1719 Schwenningen

Lauffer
Christian
* 30.03.1664 Schwenningen
† 17.03.1744 Schwenningen
⚭ 02.10.1683 Schwenningen

Palmtag
Anna Maria
* 22.02.1664 Schwenningen
† 16.12.1729 Schwenningen

Maier
Lorenz
* um 1624 Schwenningen
† 29.08.1680 Schwenningen
⚭ 1648 Schwenningen

Glaser
Maria
* um 1623 Schwenningen
† 04.11.1703 Schwenningen

Lauffer
Christian
* um 1618 Schwenningen
† 22.09.1678 Schwenningen
⚭ 24.01.1651 Schwenningen

Schlenker
Anna
* um 1615 Schwenningen
† 25.03.1675 Schwenningen

Lauffer
Jacob
* um 1622 Schwenningen
† 25.09.1674 Schwenningen
⚭ 16.06.1663 Schwenningen

> 31

Kaiser
Anna
* um 1647 Schwenningen
† 25.12.1671 Schwenningen

> 32

Palmtag
Christian
* um 1628 Schwenningen
† 08.03.1719 Schwenningen
⚭ 21.06.1656 Schwenningen

Schlenker
Anna
* um 1639 Schwenningen
† 18.01.1723 Schwenningen

Genealogical table no. 14

> 33

Kaiser
Jakob
* um 1617 Schwenningen
† 01.12.1688 Schwenningen
⚭ 5)
NN
Anna

Kaiser
Gabriel
* um 1648 Schwenningen
† 08.12.1692 Schwenningen
⚭ 22.10.1671 Schwenningen

Benzing
Jakob
* 1604 Schwenningen
† 1679 Schwenningen
⚭ 2)   vor 1639
NN
Maria
* um 1606 Schwenningen
† 27.02.1681 Schwenningen

Benzing
Katharina
* um 1646 Schwenningen
† 18.12.1714 Schwenningen

Lauffer
Christian
* um 1618 Schwenningen
† 22.09.1678 Schwenningen
⚭ 24.01.1651 Schwenningen
Schlenker
Anna
* um 1615 Schwenningen
† 25.03.1675 Schwenningen

Lauffer
Georg
* 05.05.1668 Schwenningen
† 26.08.1743 Schwenningen
⚭ 12.02.1689 Schwenningen

Würthner
Jakob
* um 1645 Schwenningen
† 25.03.1690 Schwenningen
⚭ 2)   02.11.1669 Schwenningen
Schuler
Katharina
* 1653

Würthner
Anna
* 14.10.1670 Schwenningen
† 26.03.1736 Schwenningen

Kaiser
Jakob
* 14.06.1671 Schwenningen
† 12.08.1756 Schwenningen
⚭ 08.05.1714 Schwenningen

Lauffer
Katharina
* 18.07.1696 Schwenningen
† 21.02.1764 Schwenningen

Kaiser
Georg
* 22.08.1716 Schwenningen
† 24.04.1760 Schwenningen
⚭ 2) 27.02.1753 Schwenningen

von Tafel 1
Kayser
Maria
* 23.02.1755 Schwenningen
† 24.08.1816 Schwenningen
⚭ 14.02.1775 Schwenningen

Mauthe
Jakob
* 15.01.1749 Schwenningen
† 12.08.1825 Schwenningen

Schlenker
Walpurga
* 06.01.1723 Schwenningen
† 03.03.1759 Schwenningen

Würthner
Catharina
* 10.07.1698 Schwenningen
† 30.10.1741 Schwenningen

Schlenker
Johannes
* 09.01.1693 Schwenningen
† 27.03.1755 Schwenningen
oo 2) 30.04.1720 Schwenningen

Würthner
Erhard
* 17.10.1673 Schwenningen
† 13.11.1739 Schwenningen
oo 15.06.1697 Schwenningen

Schlenker
Valentin
* 02.02.1660 Schwenningen
† 04.02.1722 Schwenningen
oo 09.05.1682 Schwenningen

Haller
Walburga
* 23.03.1655 Schwenningen
† 02.03.1731 Schwenningen

Irion
Anna
* 17.10.1674 Öfingen
† 21.03.1746 Schwenningen

Schlenker
Joseph
* um 1623 Schwenningen
† 17.12.1665 Schwenningen
oo um 1653 Schwenningen

> 34

Müller
Barbara
* um 1627 Schwenningen
† 13.10.1671 Schwenningen

> 35

Haller
Jakob
* um 1615 Schwenningen
† 17.09.1698 Schwenningen
oo 2) um 1640 Schwenningen

> 36

Lauffer
Anna
* um 1620 Schwenningen
† um 1675 Schwenningen

Würthner
Jakob
* um 1645 Schwenningen
† 25.03.1690 Schwenningen
oo 02.11.1669 Schwenningen

> 37

Schuler
Catharina
* um 1653 Schwenningen
† 15.02.1726 Schwenningen

> 38

Irion
Johann
* um 1655 Tuningen
† 20.08.1725 Tuningen
oo 17.11.1674 Tuningen

Wölflin
Agnes
* 09.05.1654 in Öfingen
† 25.08.1725 Tuningen

Genealogical table no. 15

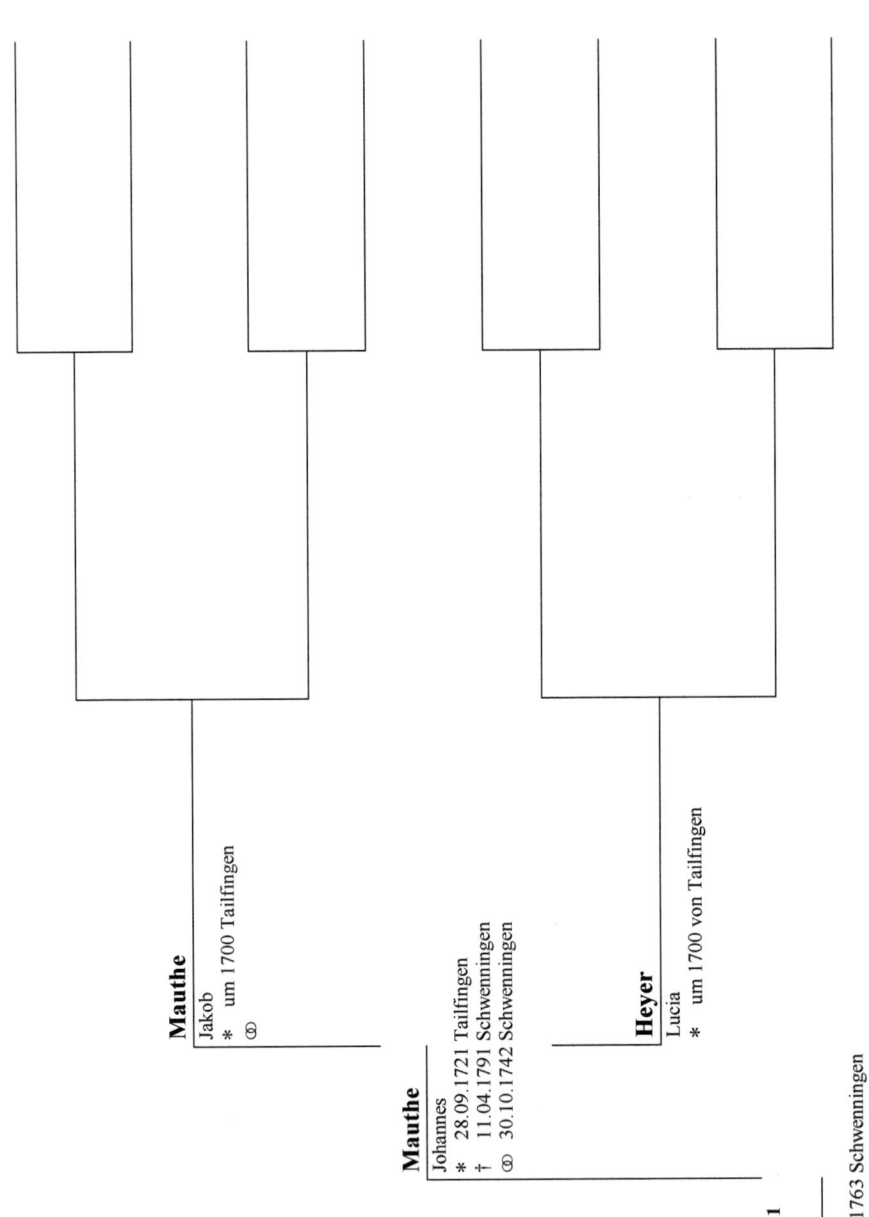

Mauthe
Jakob
* um 1700 Tailfingen
∞

Mauthe
Johannes
*   28.09.1721 Tailfingen
†   11.04.1791 Schwenningen
∞   30.10.1742 Schwenningen

Heyer
Lucia
* um 1700 von Tailfingen

von Tafel 1
Mauthe
Caspar
*   09.09.1763 Schwenningen
†   27.05.1802 Schwenningen
∞   27.07.1786 Schwenningen

Jäckle
Agnes
* 22.11.1762 Schwenningen

Maier
Christina
* 12.03.1721 Schwenningen
† 20.09.1796 Schwenningen

Maier
Christian
* 04.12.1685 Schwenningen
† 22.11.1761 Schwenningen
⚭ 28.06.1718 Schwenningen

Lauffer
Agnes
* 06.01.1696 Schwenningen

Maier
Johannes
* 05.10.1654 Schwenningen
† 04.10.1724 Schwenningen
⚭ 04.06.1676 Schwenningen

Lauffer
Agathe
* 03.12.1654 Schwenningen
† 19.02.1719 Schwenningen

Lauffer
Christian
* 30.03.1664 Schwenningen
† 17.03.1744 Schwenningen
⚭ 02.10.1683 Schwenningen

Palmtag
Anna Maria
* 22.02.1664 Schwenningen
† 16.12.1729 Schwenningen

Maier
Lorenz
* um 1624 Schwenningen
† 29.08.1680 Schwenningen
⚭ 1648 Schwenningen

Glaser
Maria
* um 1623 Schwenningen
† 04.11.1703 Schwenningen

Lauffer
Christian
* um 1618 Schwenningen
† 22.09.1678 Schwenningen
⚭ 24.01.1651 Schwenningen

Schlenker
Anna
* um 1615 Schwenningen
† 25.03.1675 Schwenningen

Lauffer
Jacob
* um 1622 Schwenningen
† 25.09.1674 Schwenningen
⚭ 16.06.1663 Schwenningen
> 39

Kaiser
Anna
* um 1647 Schwenningen
† 25.12.1671 Schwenningen

Palmtag
Christian
* um 1628 Schwenningen
† 08.03.1719 Schwenningen
⚭ 21.06.1656 Schwenningen
> 40

Schlenker
Anna
* um 1639 Schwenningen
† 18.01.1723 Schwenningen

Genealogical table no. 16

Jäckle
Jakob
* um 1649 Schwenningen
† 26.03.1707 Schwenningen
∞ 22.04.1673 Schwenningen

Benzing
Margaretha
* 24.02.1654 Schwenningen
† 06.10.1722 Schwenningen

Haller
Jakob
* um 1640 in Trossingen
∞

Jäckle
Jakob
* 01.05.1676 Schwenningen
† 04.11.1731 Schwenningen
∞ 13.06.1702 Schwenningen

Haller
Christina
* um 1662 von Trossingen
† 16.04.1710 Schwenningen

Vosseler
Johannes
* 22.03.1684 Schwenningen
† 20.05.1759 Schwenningen
∞ 21.10.1704 Schwenningen

Schuler
Agnes
* 08.08.1684 Schwenningen
† 17.02.1751 Schwenningen

Jäckle
Jakob
* 03.05.1707 Schwenningen
† 18.05.1785 Schwenningen
∞ 30.04.1736 Schwenningen

Vosseler
Agnes
* 26.11.1710 Schwenningen
† 09.01.1775 Schwenningen

Jäckle
Jakob
* 24.05.1739 Schwenningen
† 21.03.1819 Schwenningen
∞ 27.01.1761 Schwenningen

von Tafel 1
Jäckle
Agnes
* 22.11.1762 Schwenningen
∞ 27.07.1786 Schwenningen

Mauthe
Caspar
* 09.09.1763 Schwenningen
† 27.05.1802 Schwenningen

Benzing
Eva Christina
* 13.03.1740 Schwenningen
† 05.10.1791 Schwenningen

Benzing
Christian
* 16.12.1714 Schwenningen
† 12.05.1805 Schwenningen
⚭ 19.11.1737 Schwenningen

Schneckenburger
Maria
* 14.04.1716 von Biesingen
† 28.09.1796 Schwenningen

Benzing
Christian
* 05.03.1691 Schwenningen
† 10.01.1775 Schwenningen
⚭ 04.01.1710 Schwenningen

Kautt
Eva Christina
* 21.08.1687 Trossingen
† 17.05.1761 Schwenningen

Schneckenburger
Hans Jakob
* um 1690
⚭

Nopper
Anna
* um 1690

Benzing
Christian
* 17.02.1660 Schwenningen
† 30.01.1738 Schwenningen
⚭ 17.06.1679 Schwenningen

Kohler
Maria
* 00.06.1652 Trossingen
† 21.04.1733 Schwenningen

Kautt
Christian
* um 1660 Trossingen
⚭

Genealogical table no. 17

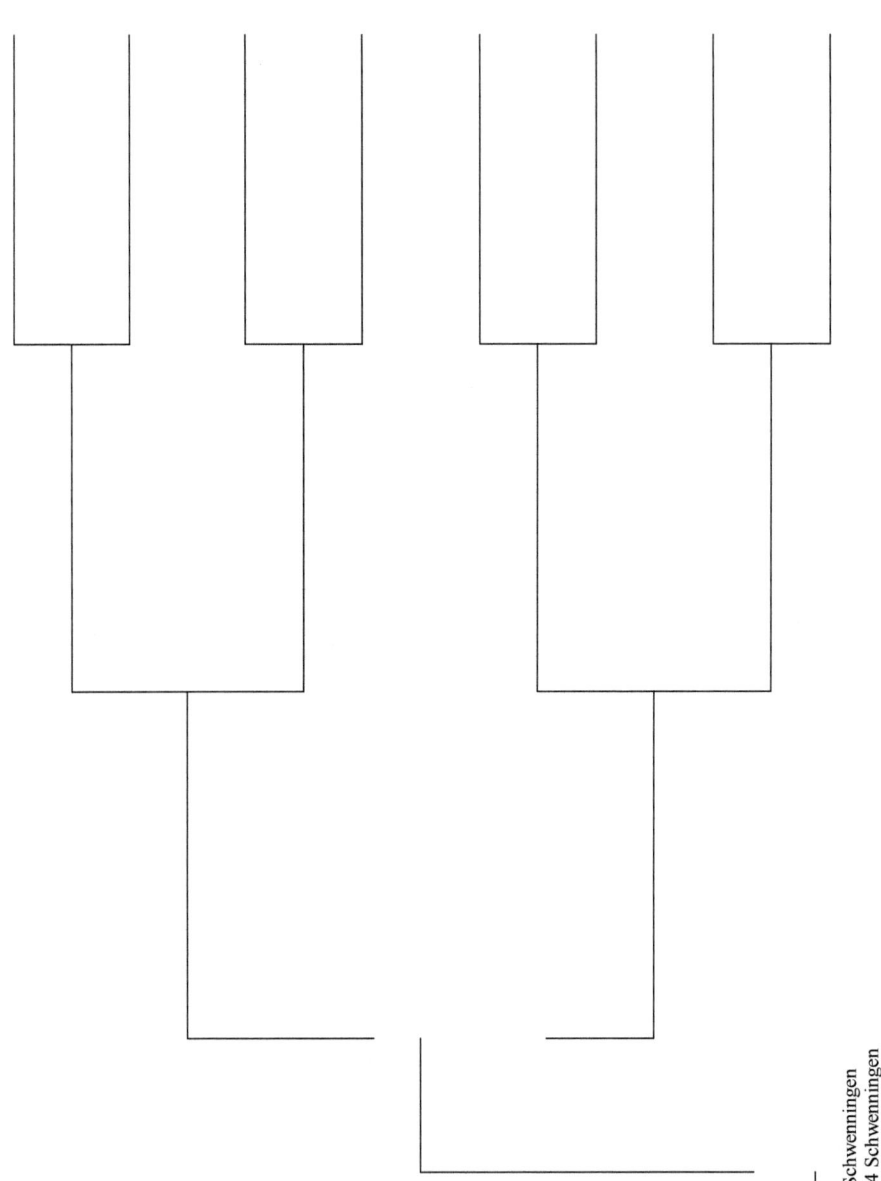

von Tafel 4
Lauffer

Jacob
* um 1622 Schwenningen
† 25.09.1674 Schwenningen
⊕ 16.06.1663 Schwenningen

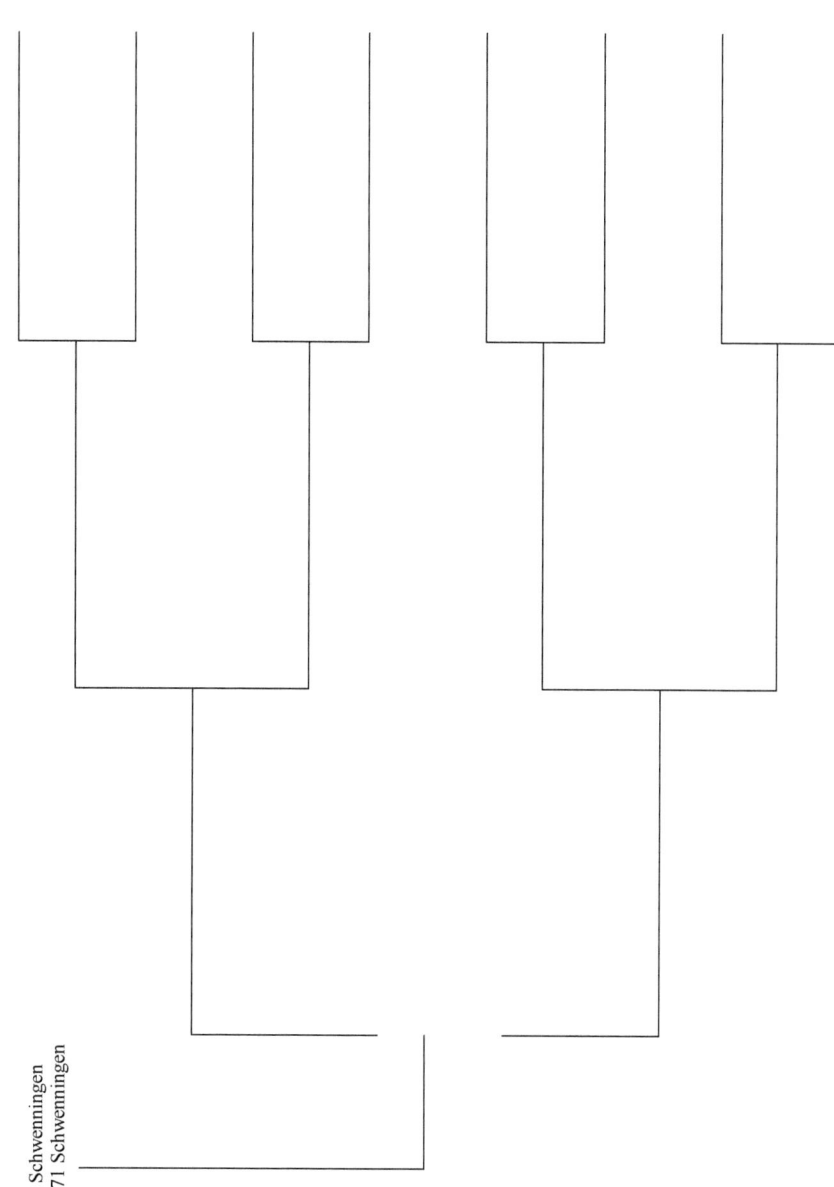

Kaiser
Anna
* um 1647 Schwenningen
† 25.12.1671 Schwenningen

Genealogical table no. 18

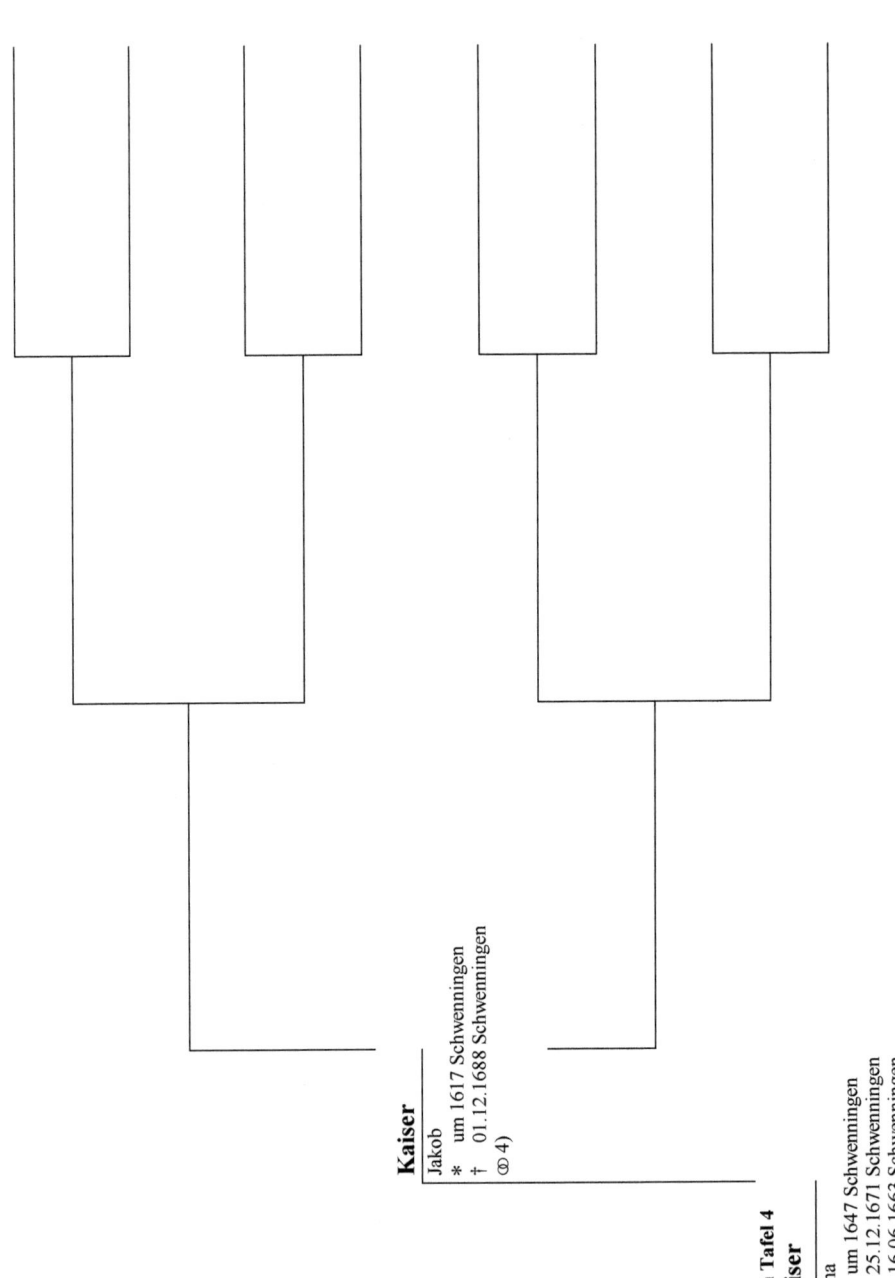

Kaiser
Jakob
* um 1617 Schwenningen
† 01.12.1688 Schwenningen
⚭ 4)

von Tafel 4
Kaiser
Anna
* um 1647 Schwenningen
† 25.12.1671 Schwenningen
⚭ 16.06.1663 Schwenningen

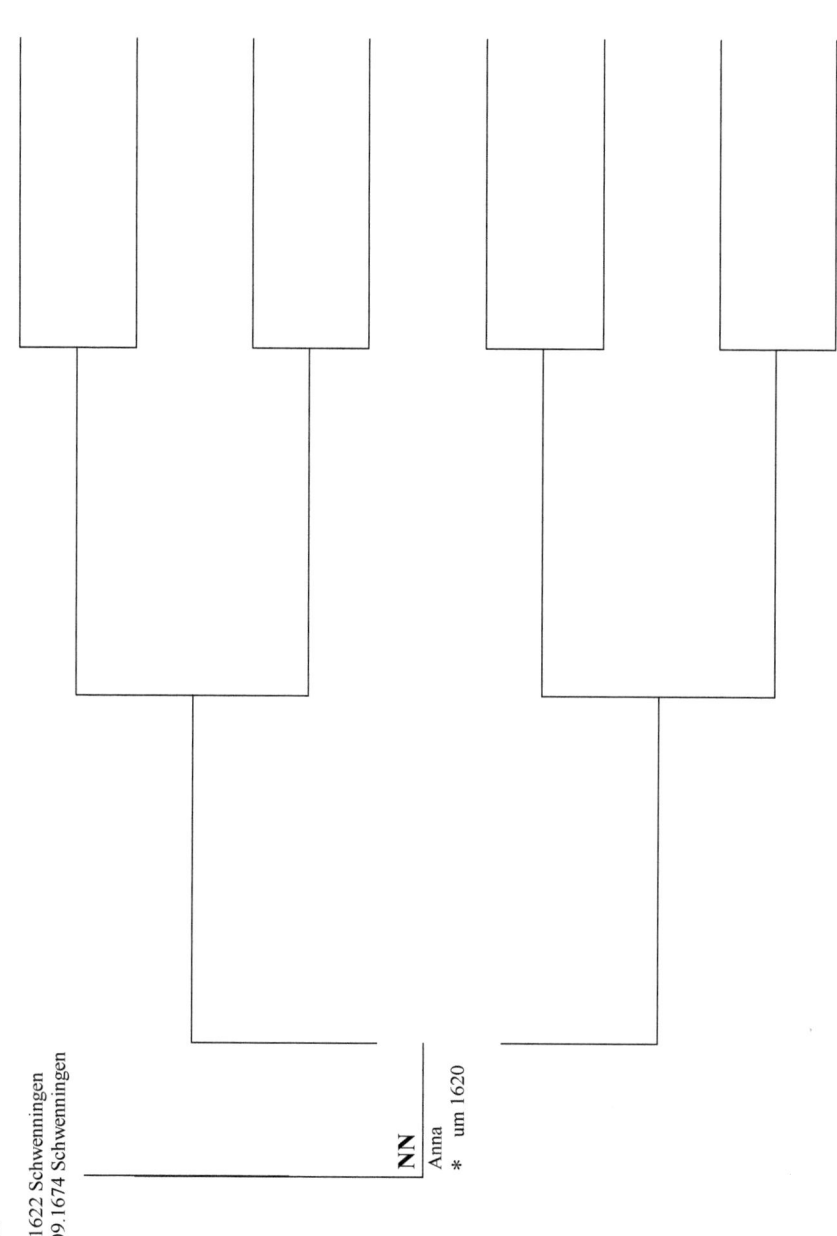

Lauffer
Jacob
* um 1622 Schwenningen
† 25.09.1674 Schwenningen

NN
Anna
* um 1620

Genealogical table no. 19

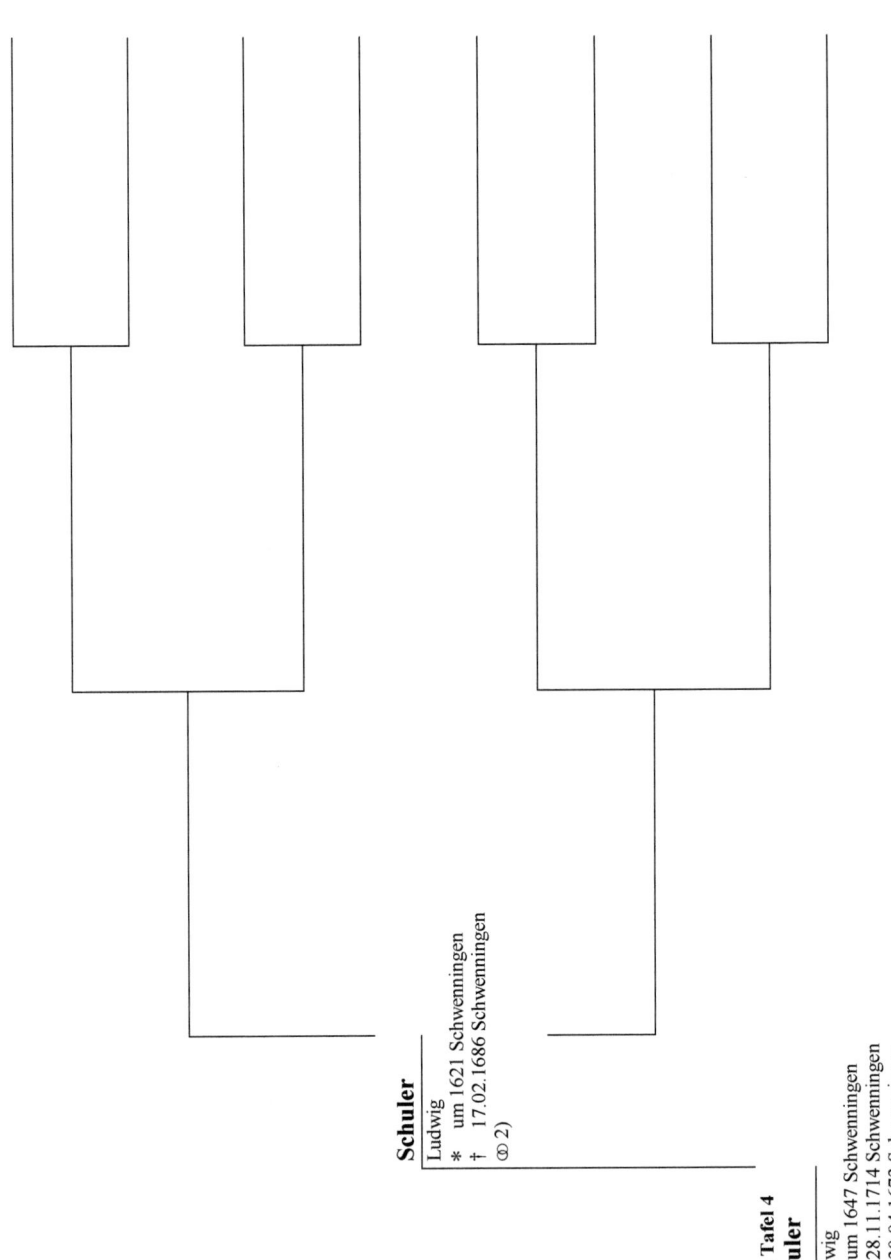

Schuler
Ludwig
* um 1621 Schwenningen
† 17.02.1686 Schwenningen
⚭ 2)

von Tafel 4
Schuler
Ludwig
* um 1647 Schwenningen
† 28.11.1714 Schwenningen
⚭ 30.04.1673 Schwenningen

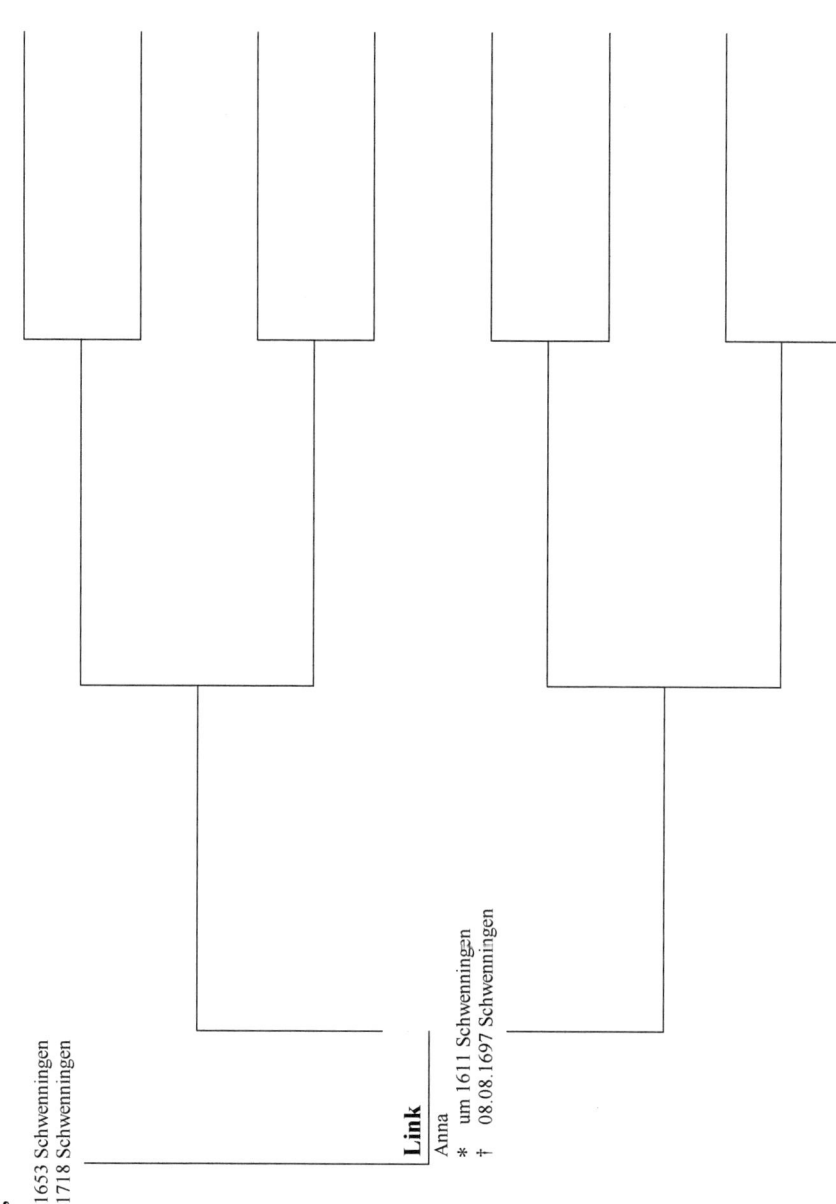

Benzing
Agathe
* 07.02.1653 Schwenningen
† 05.01.1718 Schwenningen

Link
Anna
* um 1611 Schwenningen
† 08.08.1697 Schwenningen

Genealogical table no. 20

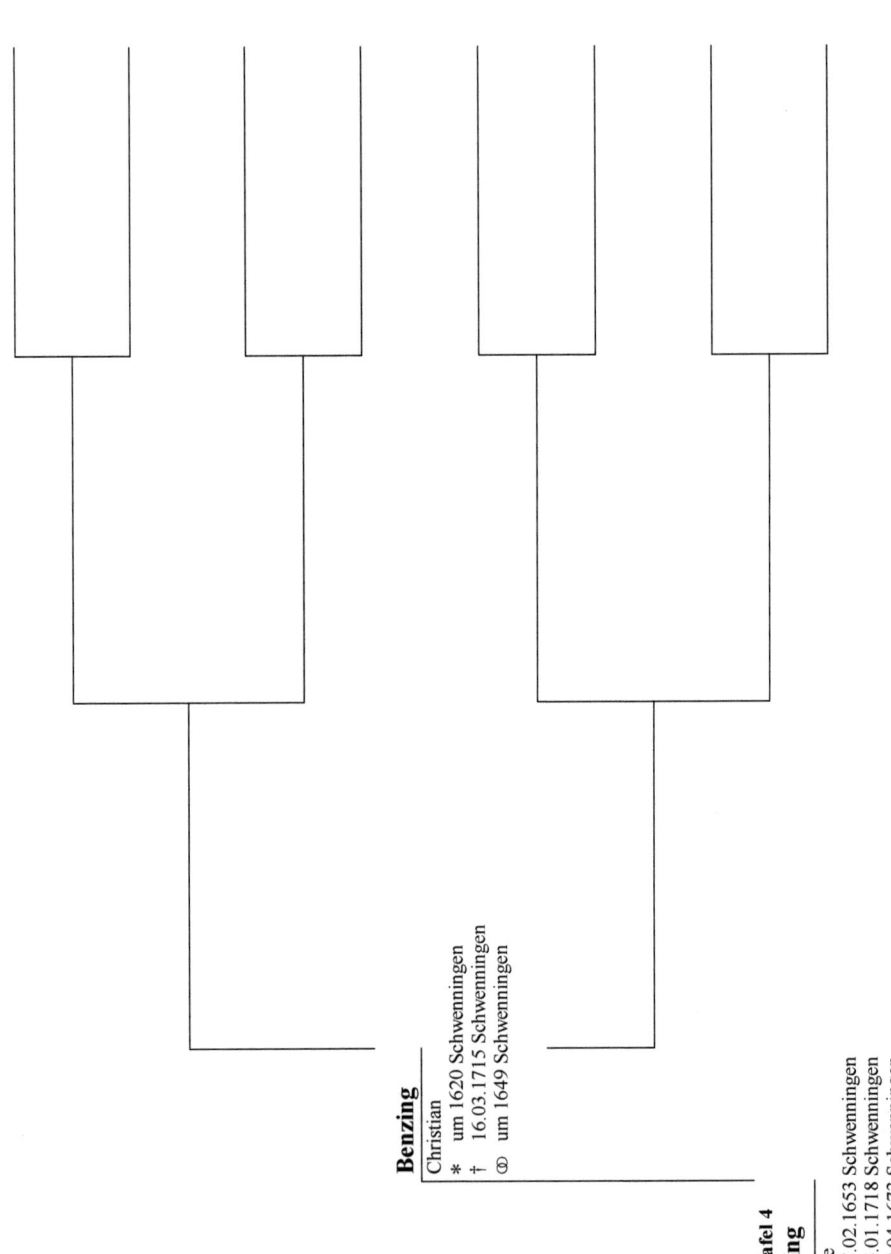

Benzing

Christian

*   um 1620 Schwenningen

†   16.03.1715 Schwenningen

⚭   um 1649 Schwenningen

von Tafel 4

Benzing

Agathe

*   07.02.1653 Schwenningen

†   05.01.1718 Schwenningen

⚭   30.04.1673 Schwenningen

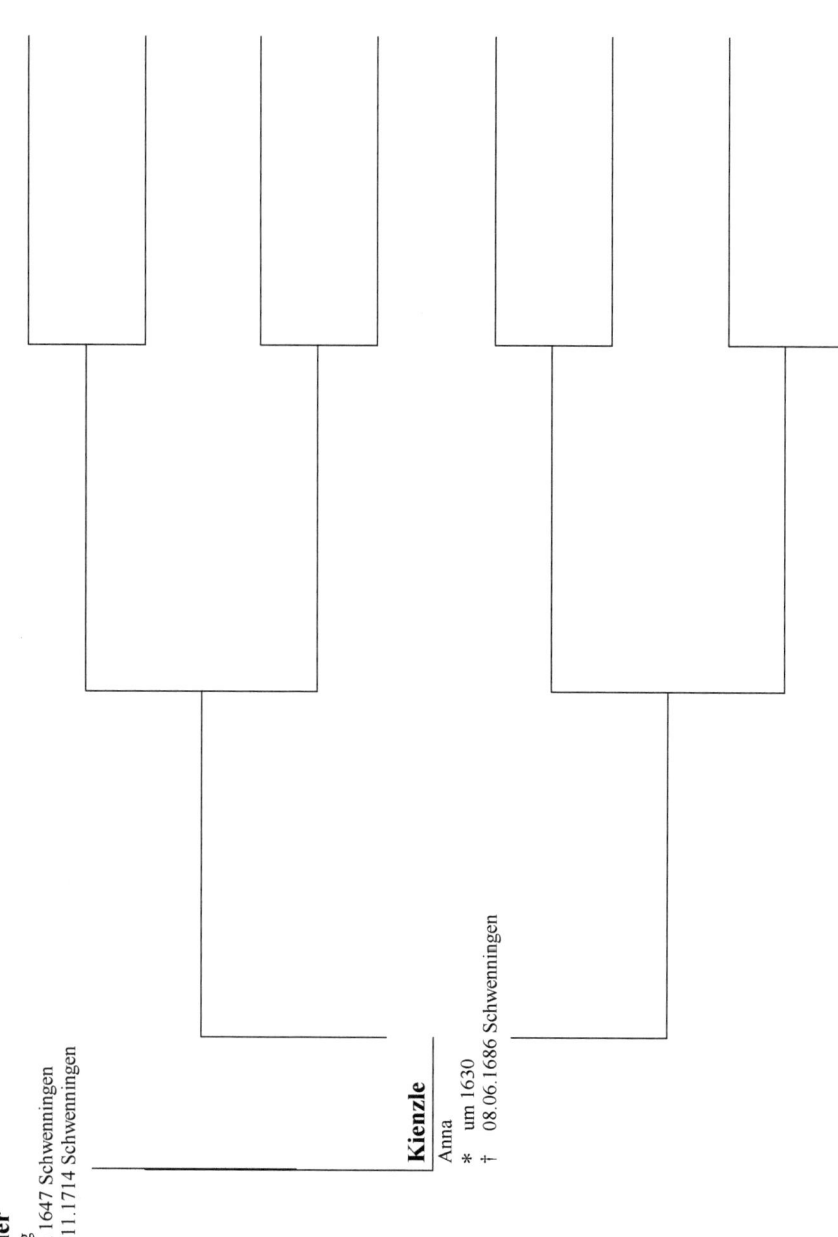

Schuler
Ludwig
* um 1647 Schwenningen
† 28.11.1714 Schwenningen

Kienzle
Anna
* um 1630
† 08.06.1686 Schwenningen

Genealogical table no. 21

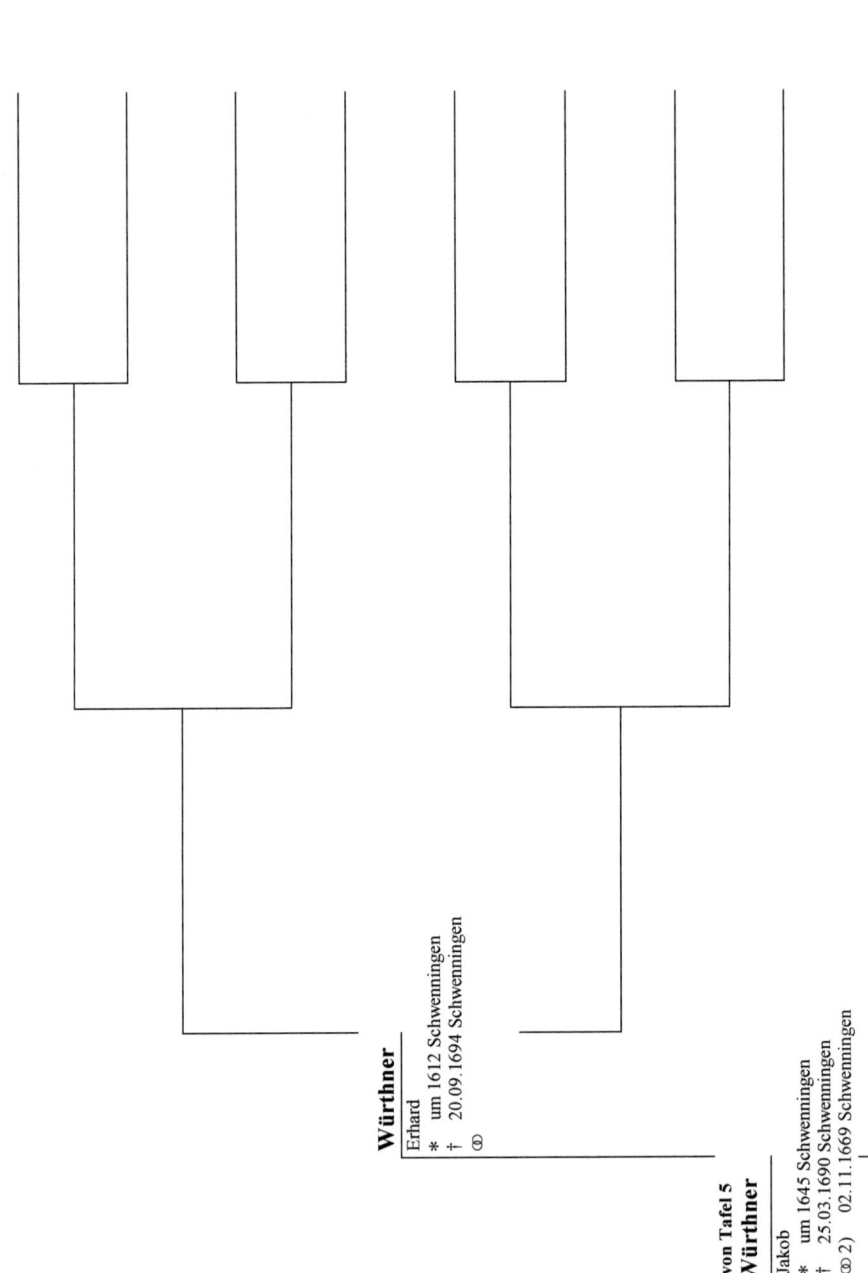

Würthner

Erhard

* um 1612 Schwenningen

† 20.09.1694 Schwenningen

⚭

von Tafel 5
Würthner

Jakob

* um 1645 Schwenningen

† 25.03.1690 Schwenningen

⚭ 2) 02.11.1669 Schwenningen

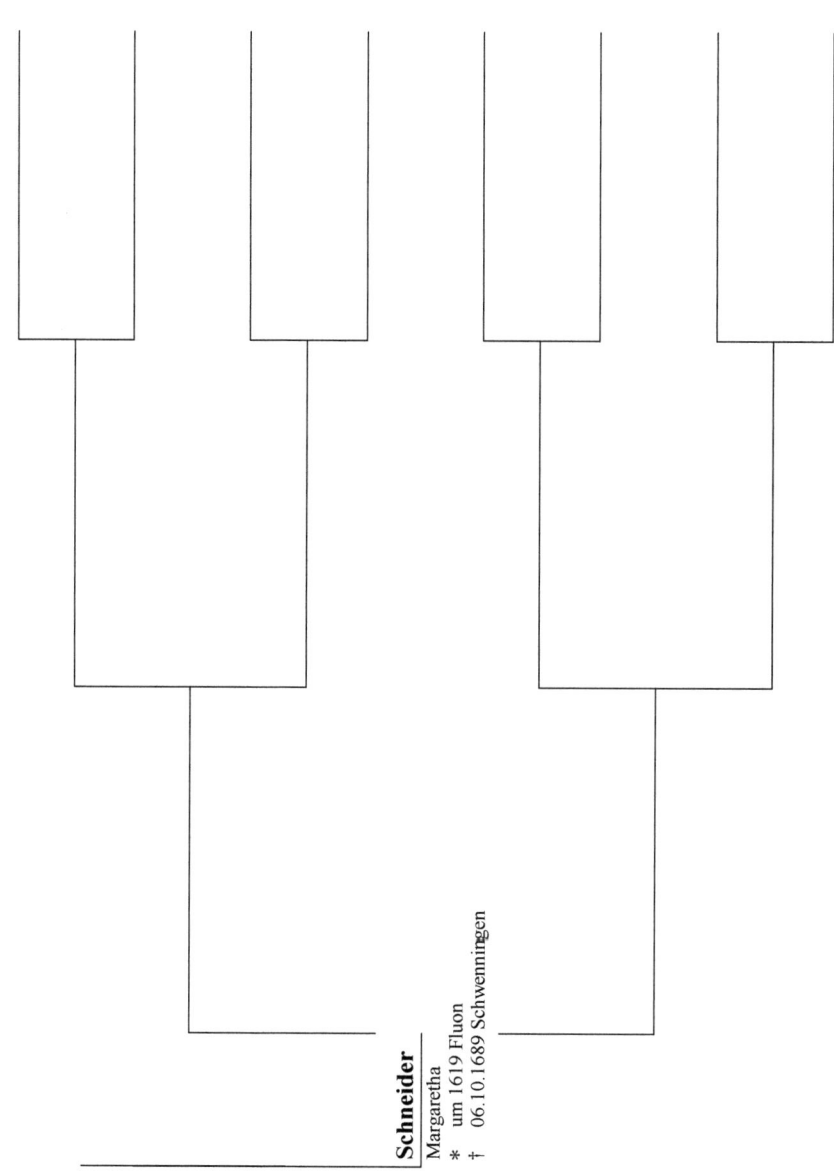

Schuler
Katharina
* 1653

Schneider
Margaretha
* um 1619 Fluon
† 06.10.1689 Schwenningen

Genealogical table no. 22

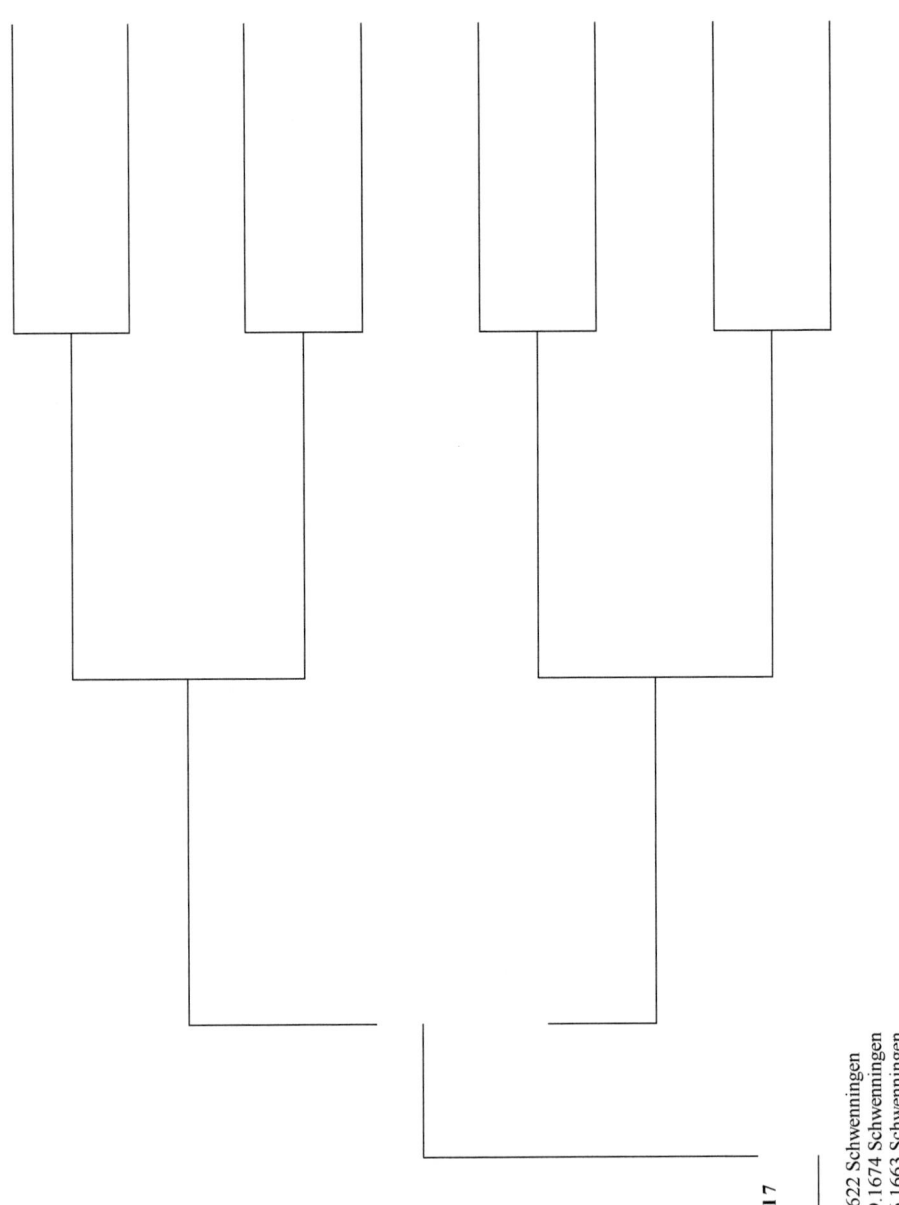

von Tafel 7
Lauffer

Jacob
* um 1622 Schwenningen
† 25.09.1674 Schwenningen
⚭ 16.06.1663 Schwenningen

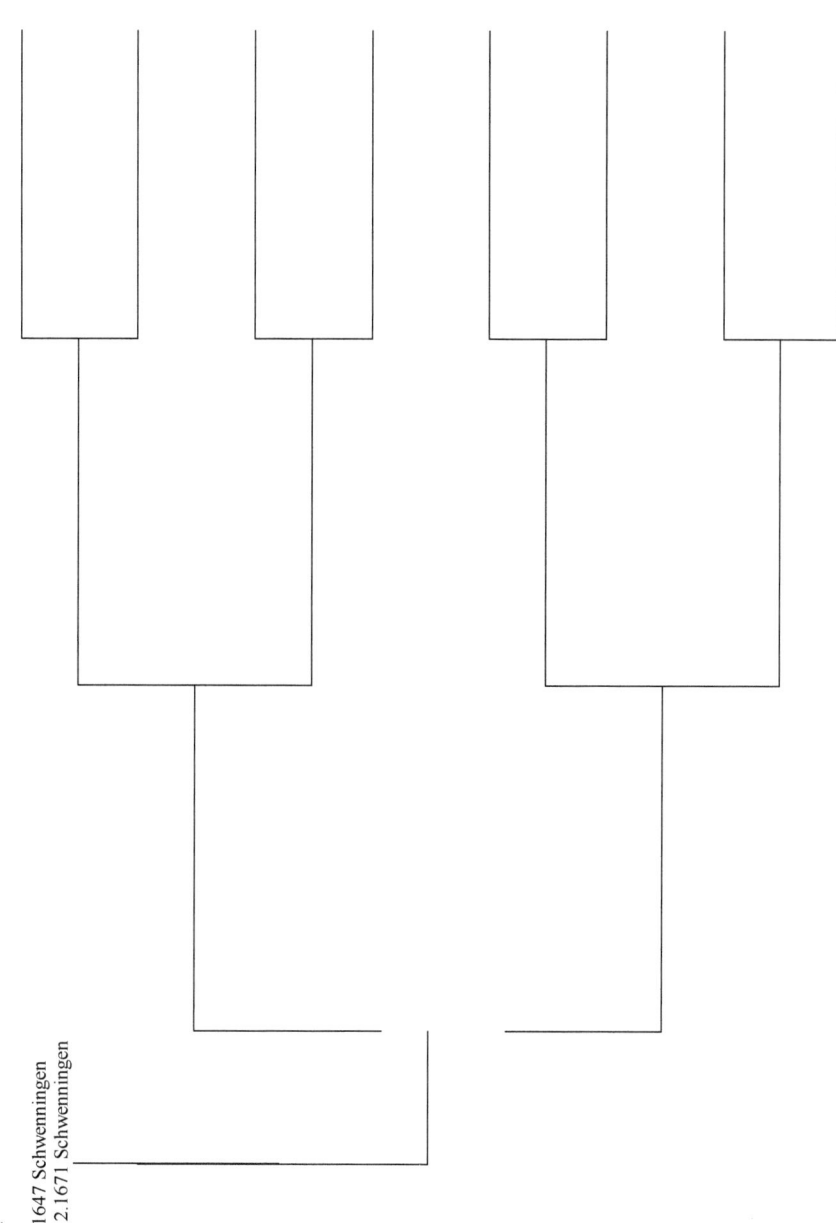

Kaiser
Anna
* um 1647 Schwenningen
† 25.12.1671 Schwenningen

Genealogical table no. 23

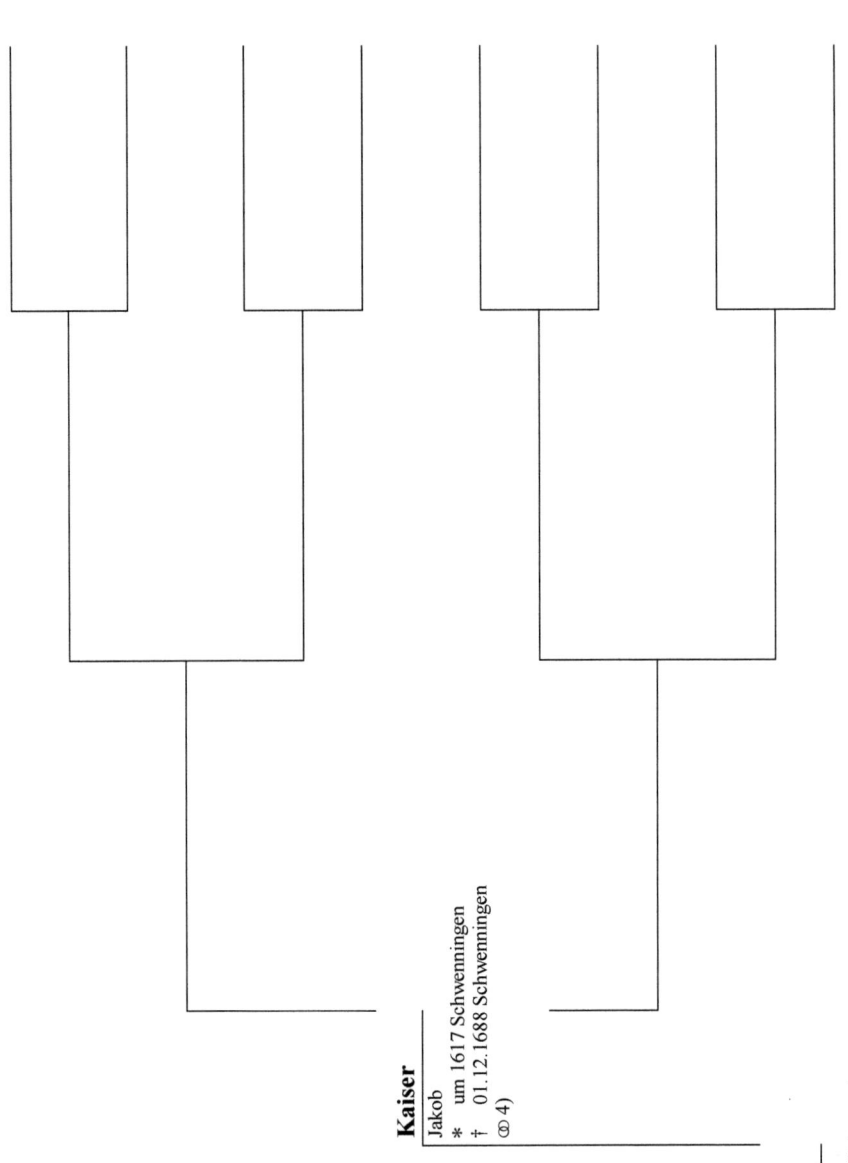

Kaiser

Jakob
* um 1617 Schwenningen
† 01.12.1688 Schwenningen
⚭ 4)

von Tafel 7
Kaiser

Anna
* um 1647 Schwenningen
† 25.12.1671 Schwenningen
⚭ 16.06.1663 Schwenningen

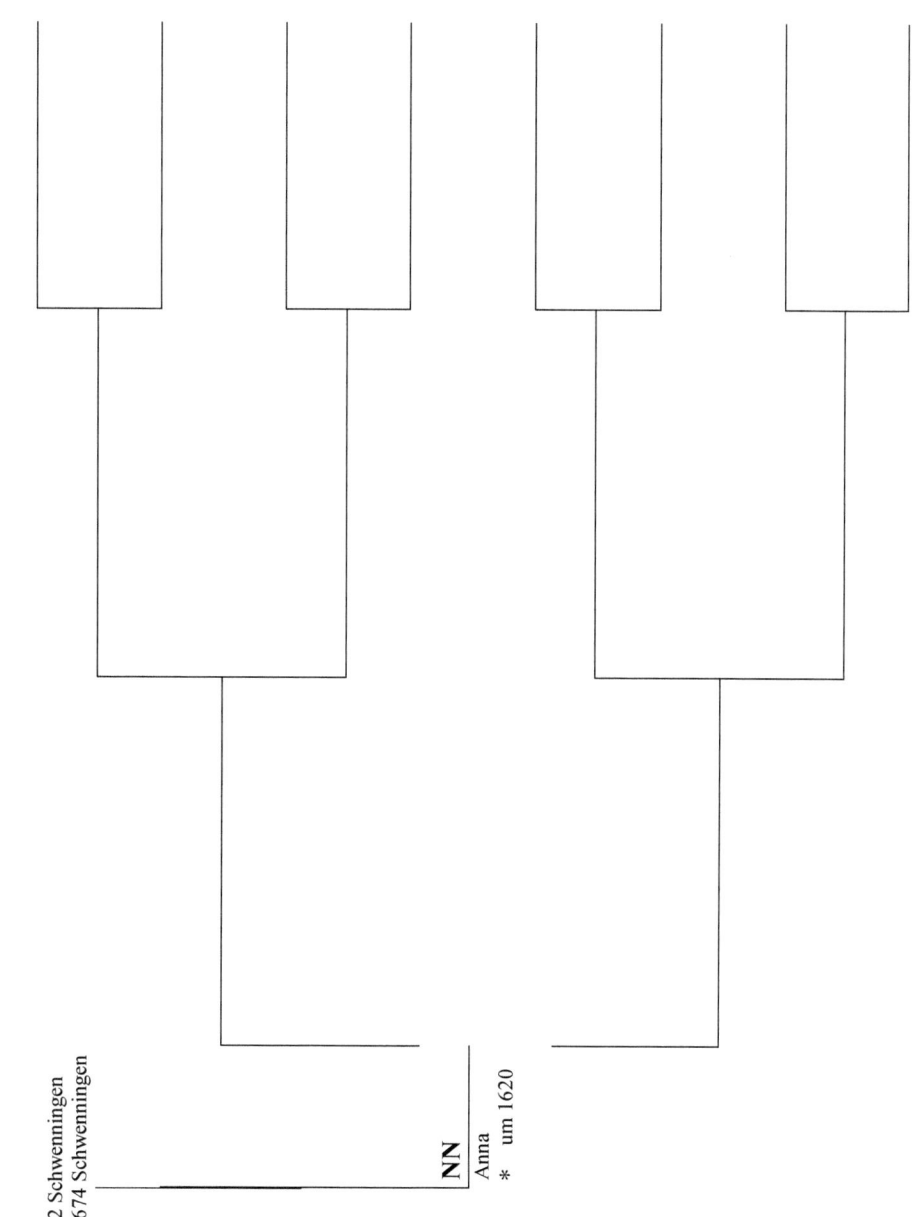

Lauffer
Jacob
* um 1622 Schwenningen
† 25.09.1674 Schwenningen

NN
Anna
* um 1620

Genealogical table no. 23

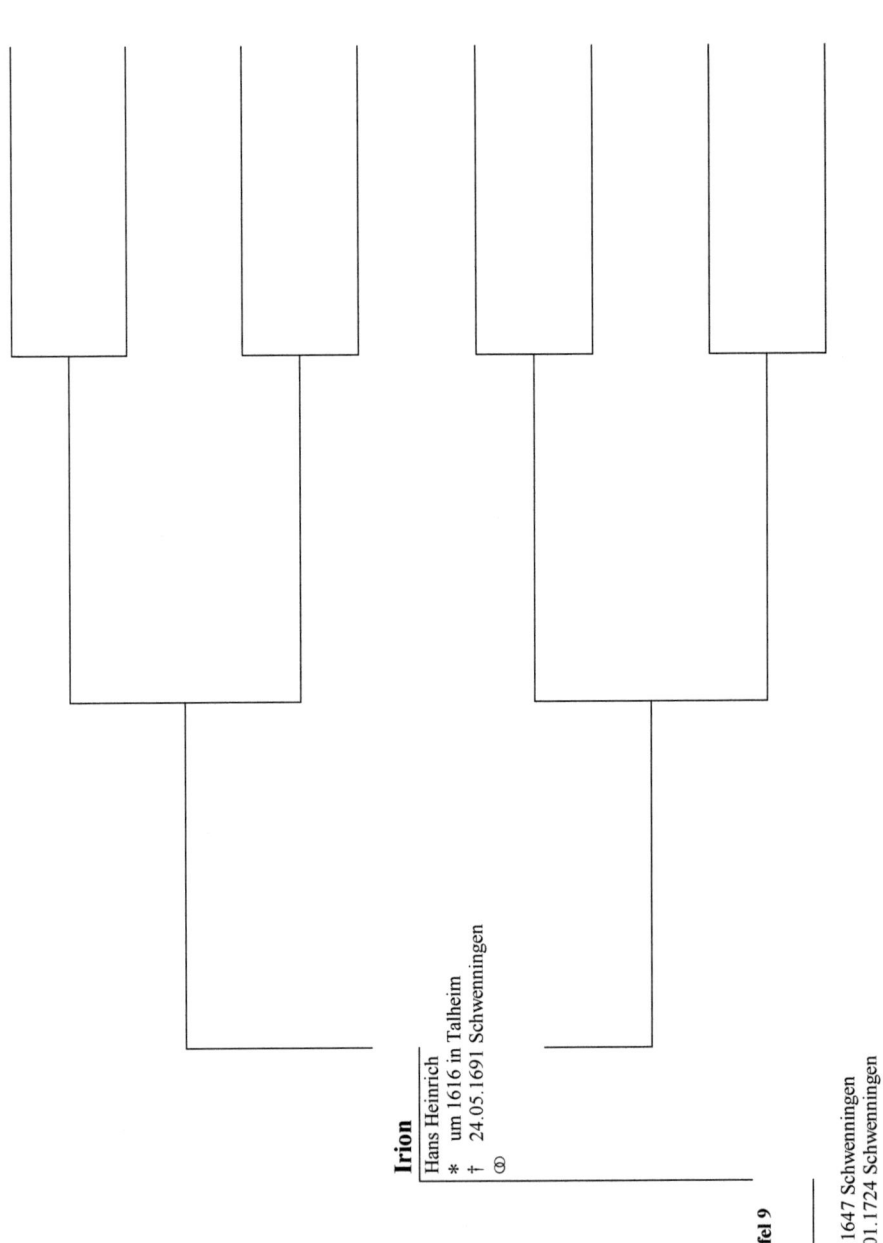

Irion
Hans Heinrich
* um 1616 in Talheim
† 24.05.1691 Schwenningen
⚭

von Tafel 9
Irion
Maria
* um 1647 Schwenningen
† 31.01.1724 Schwenningen
⚭ 26.09.1671 Schwenningen

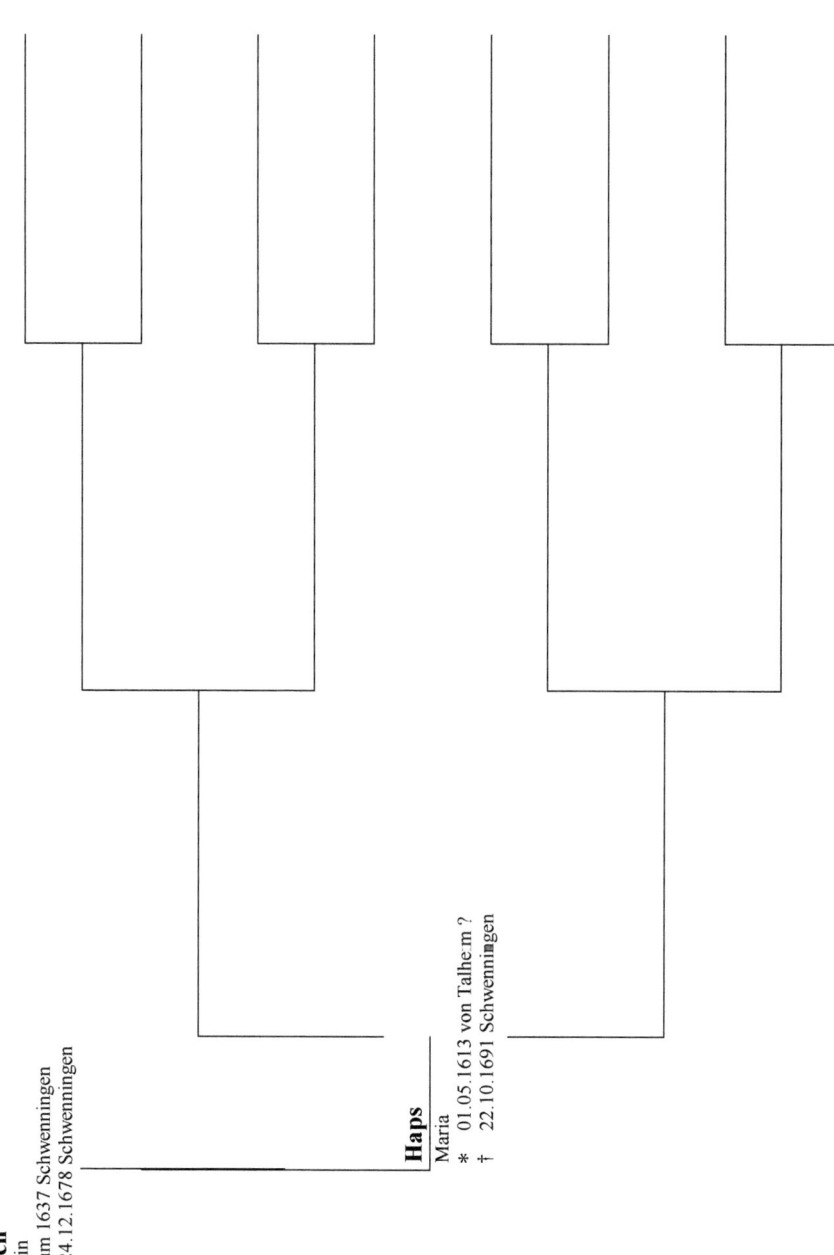

Jauch
Martin
* um 1637 Schwenningen
† 24.12.1678 Schwenningen

Haps
Maria
* 01.05.1613 von Talheim ?
† 22.10.1691 Schwenningen

Genealogical table no. 25

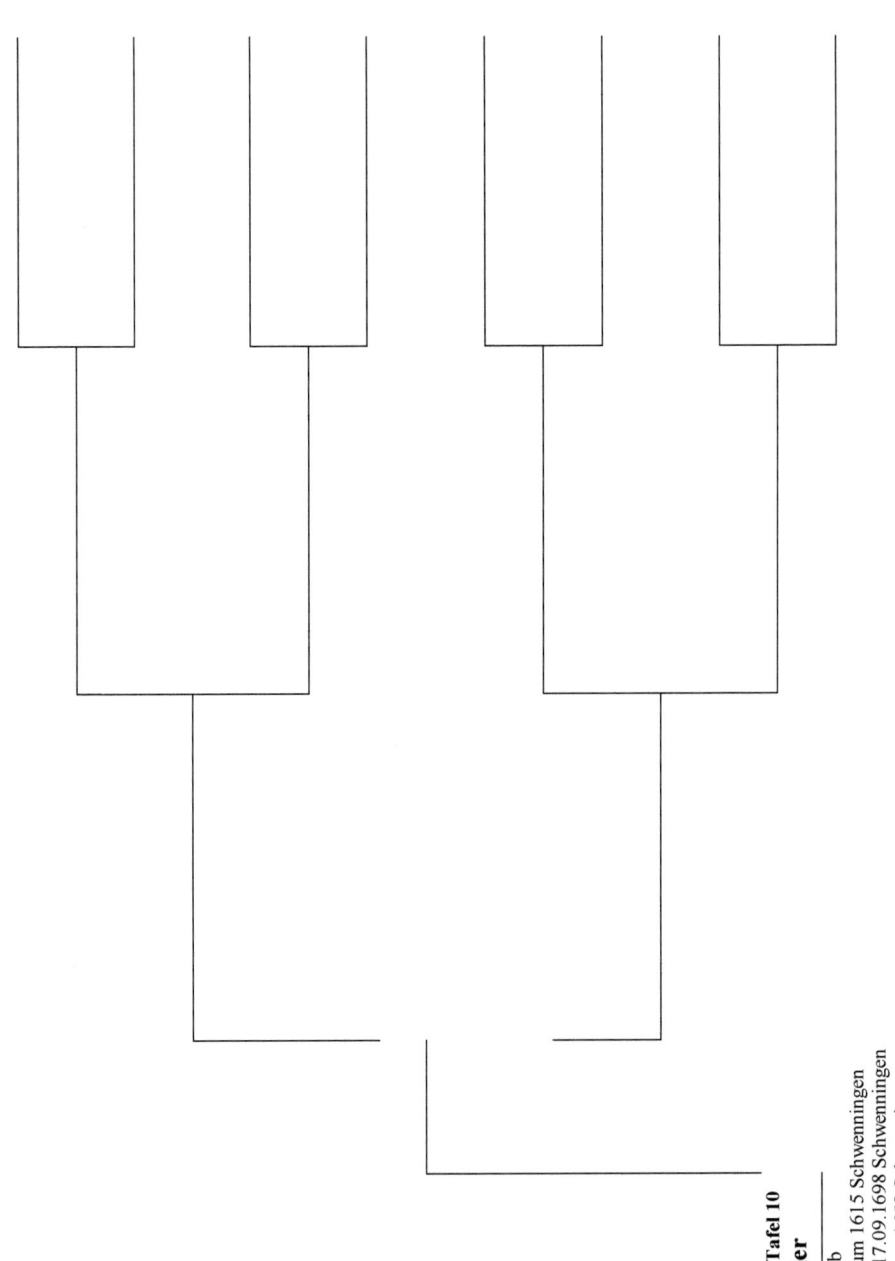

von Tafel 10
Haller

Jakob
* um 1615 Schwenningen
† 17.09.1698 Schwenningen
∞ um 1652 Schwenningen

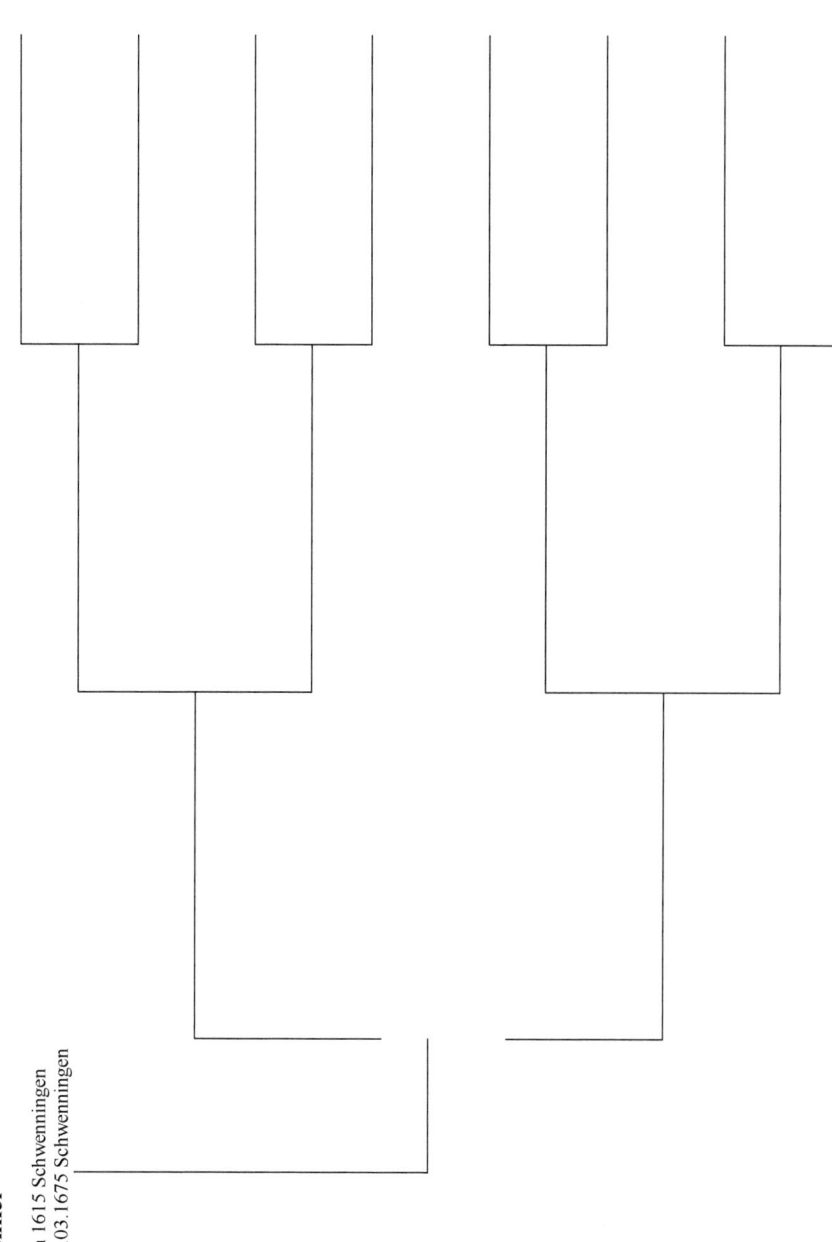

Schlenker
Anna
* um 1615 Schwenningen
† 25.03.1675 Schwenningen

Genealogical table no. 26

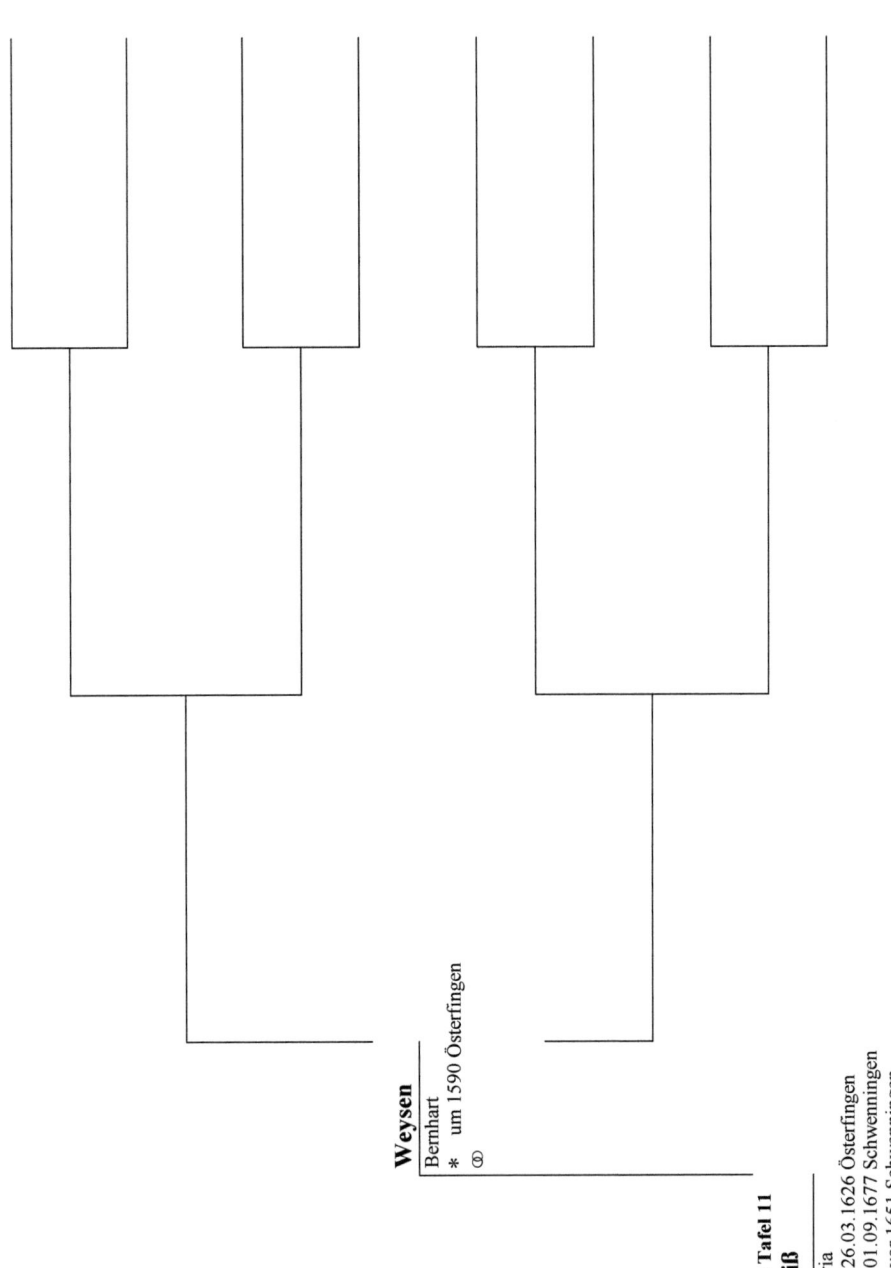

Weysen
Bernhart
* um 1590 Österfingen
⚭

von Tafel 11
Weiß
Maria
* 26.03.1626 Österfingen
† 01.09.1677 Schwenningen
⚭ vor 1651 Schwenningen

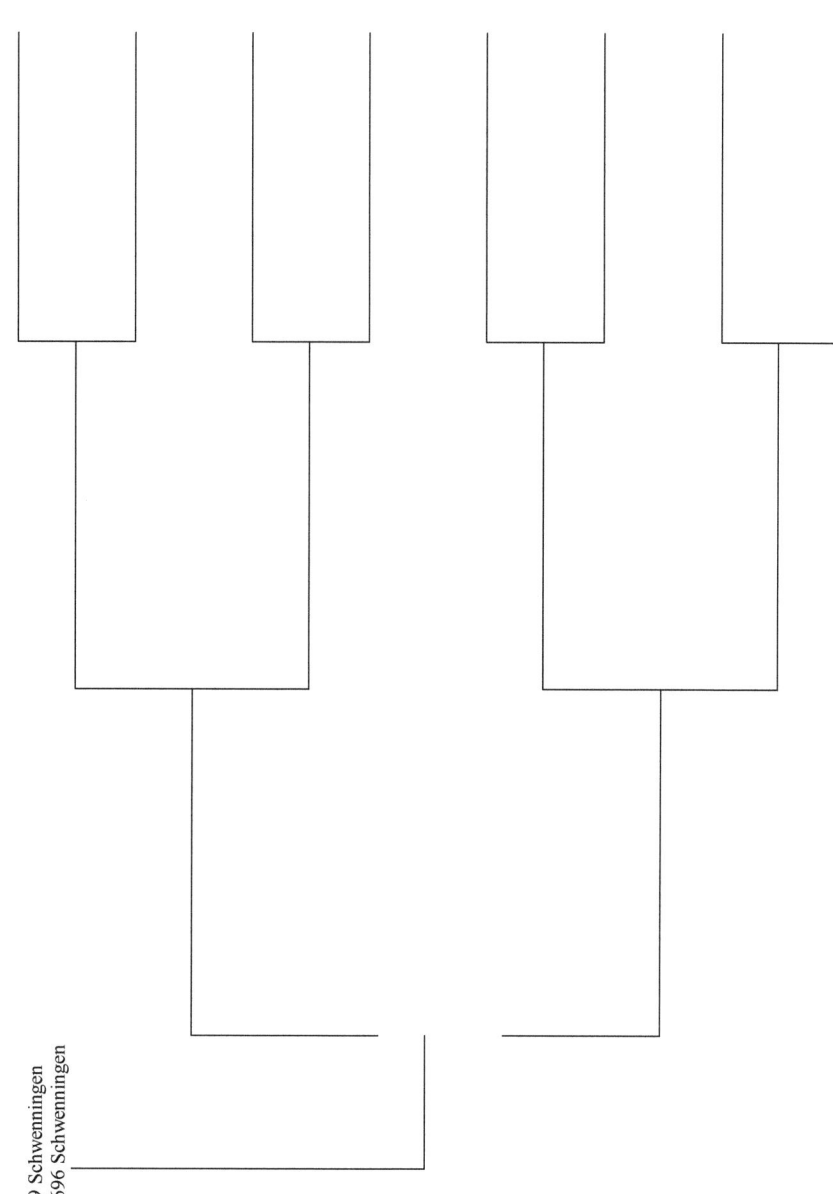

Rapp
Conrad
* um 1629 Schwenningen
† 12.03.1696 Schwenningen

Genealogical table no. 27

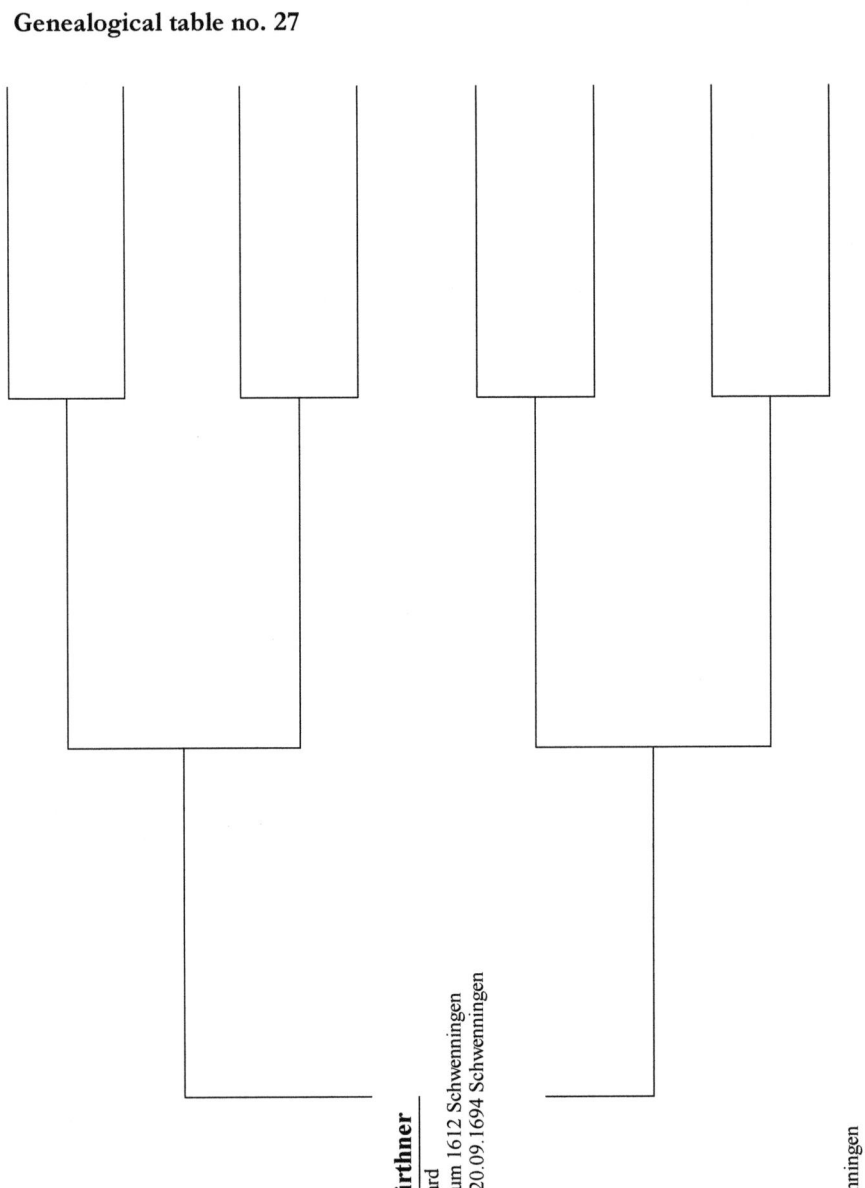

Würthner

Erhard
* um 1612 Schwenningen
† 20.09.1694 Schwenningen
⚭

von Tafel 11
Würthner

Jakob
* um 1645 Schwenningen
† 25.03.1690 Schwenningen
⚭ 2) 02.11.1669 Schwenningen

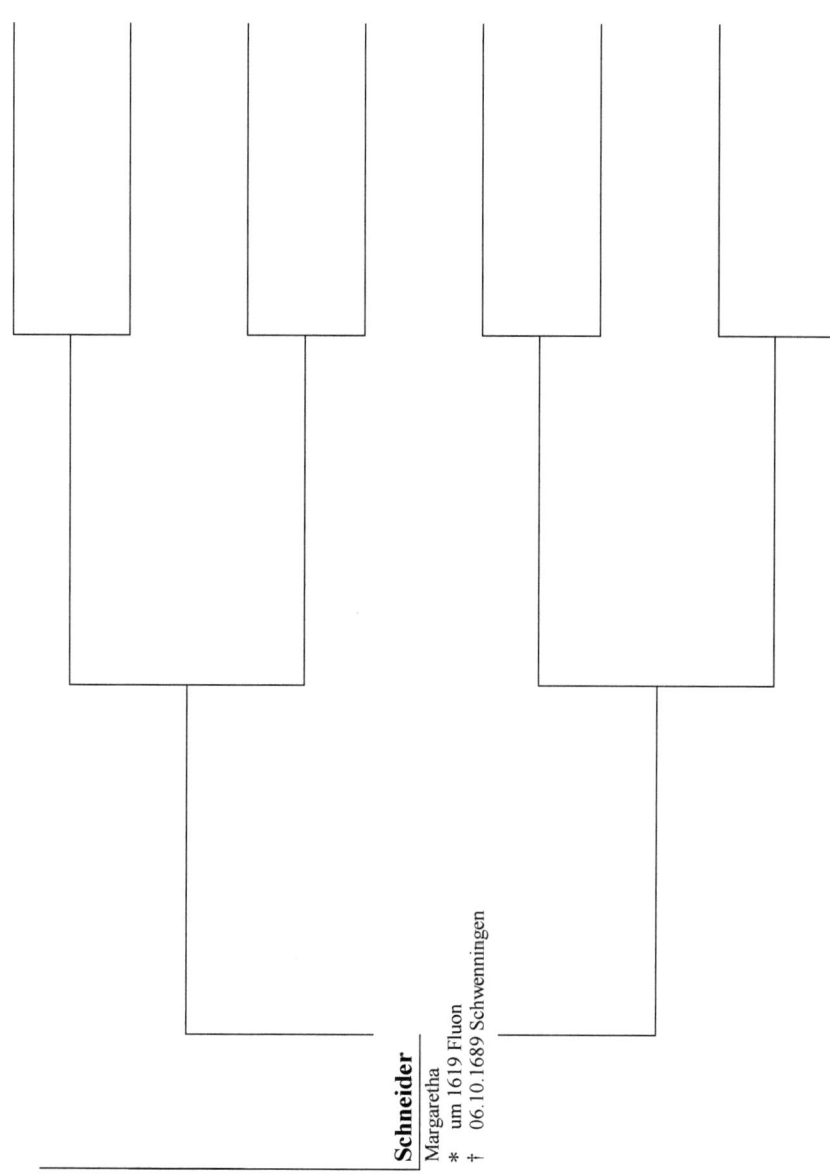

Schuler
Katharina
* 1653

Schneider
Margaretha
* um 1619 Fluon
† 06.10.1689 Schwenningen

Genealogical table no. 28

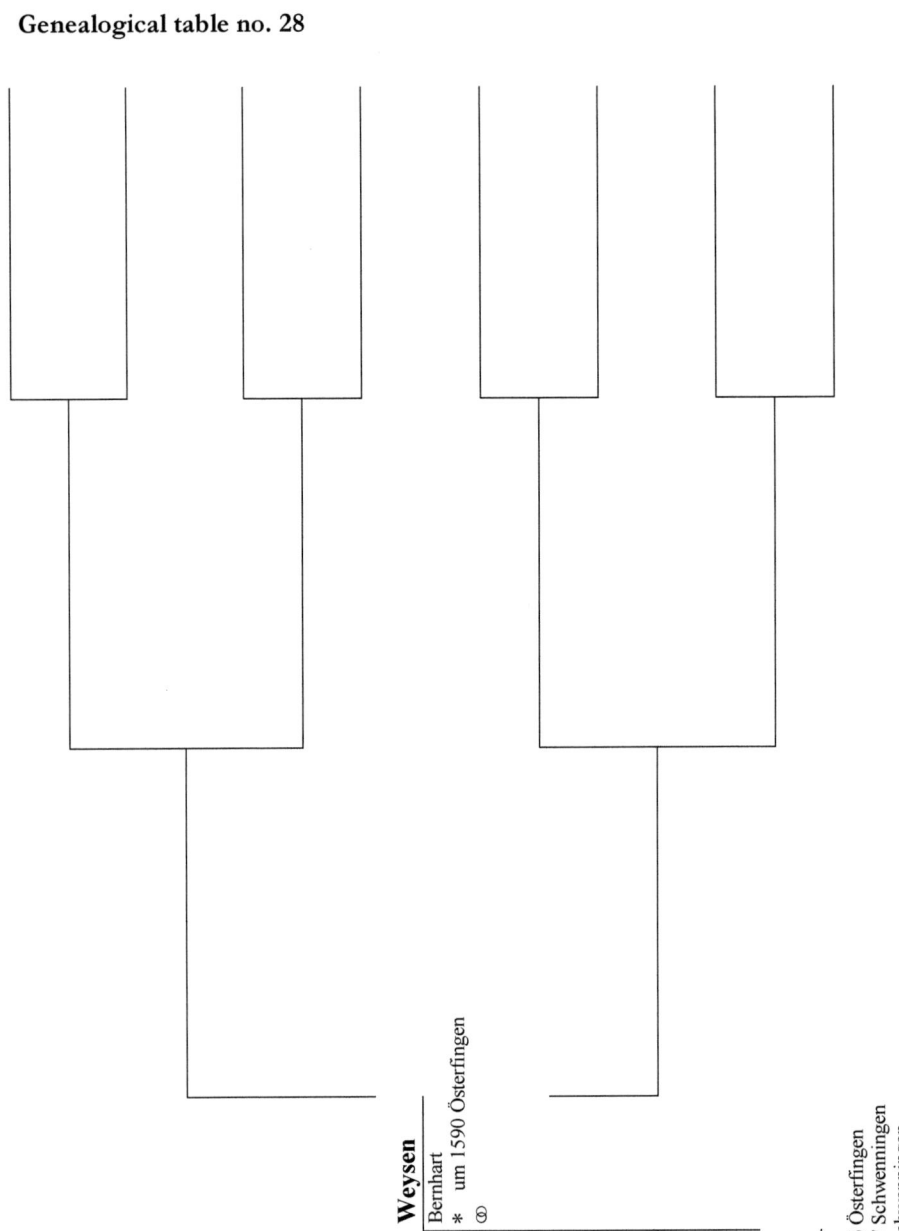

Weysen
Bernhart
* um 1590 Österfingen
∞

von Tafel 12
Weiß
Maria
* 26.03.1626 Österfingen
† 01.09.1677 Schwenningen
∞ vor 1651 Schwenningen

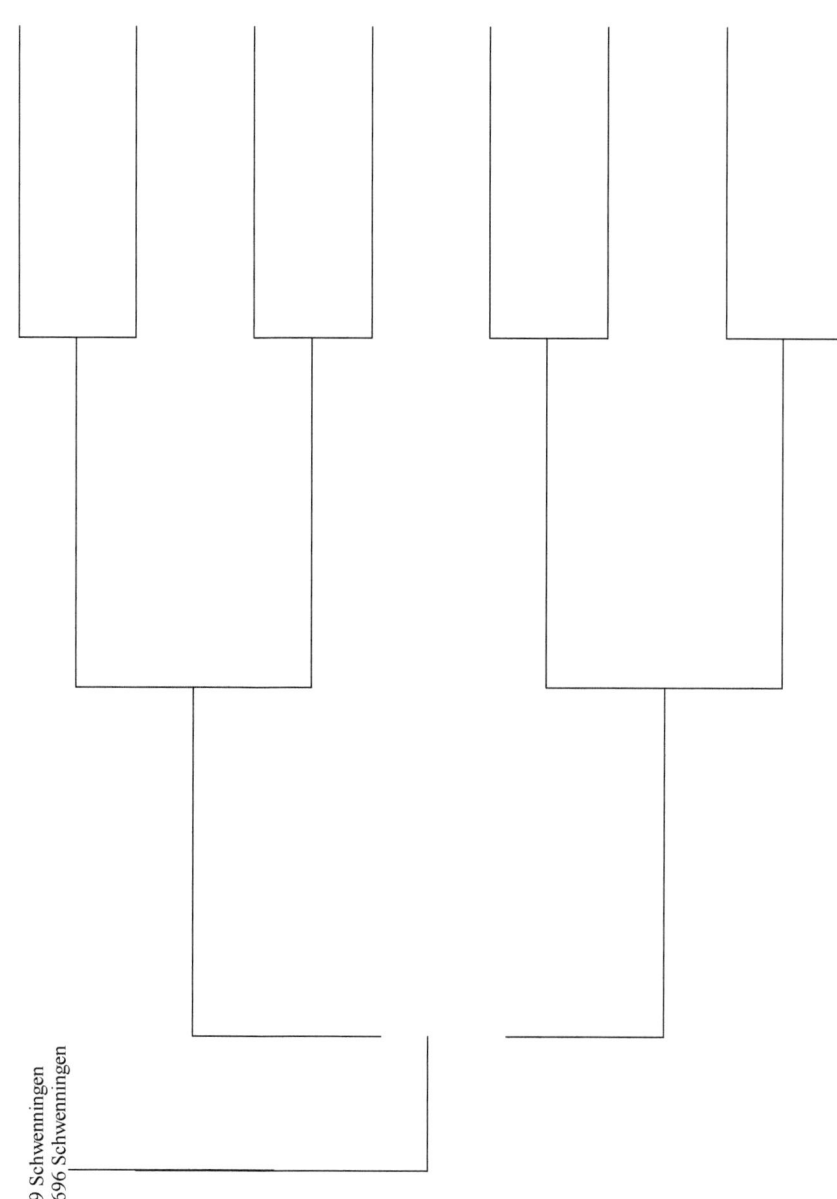

Rapp
Conrad
* um 1629 Schwenningen
† 12.03.1696 Schwenningen

Genealogical table no. 29

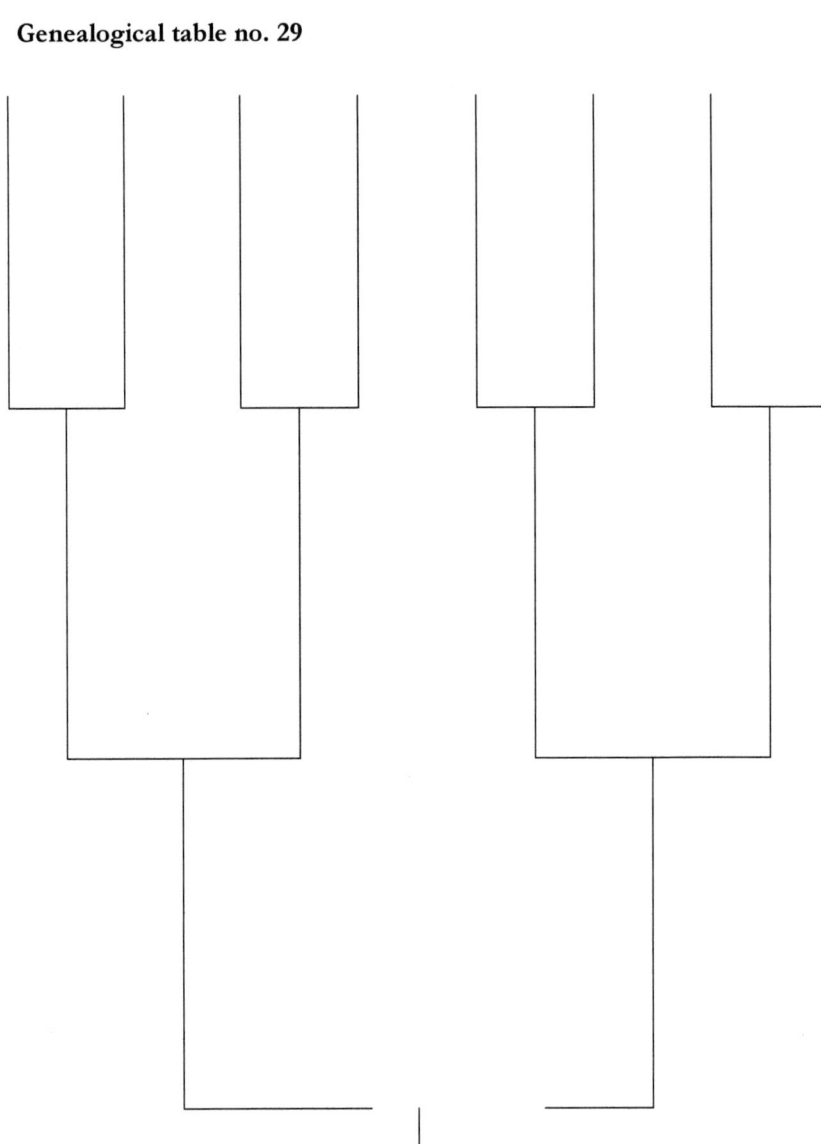

von Tafel 12
Link

Jakob
*   05.09.1641 von Schura
†   30.01.1690 Schwenningen
⚭ 2)   31.01.1665 Schwenningen

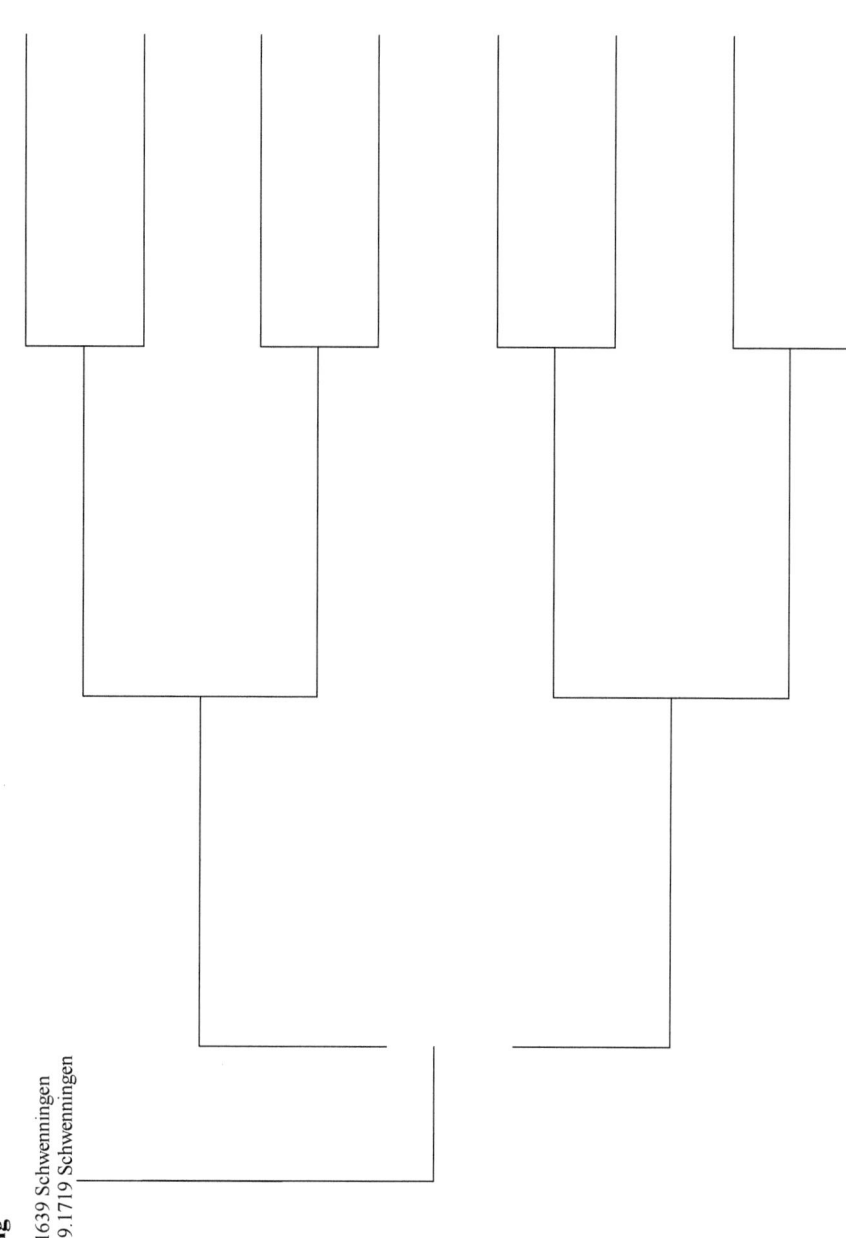

Benzing
Anna
* um 1639 Schwenningen
† 01.09.1719 Schwenningen

Genealogical table no. 30

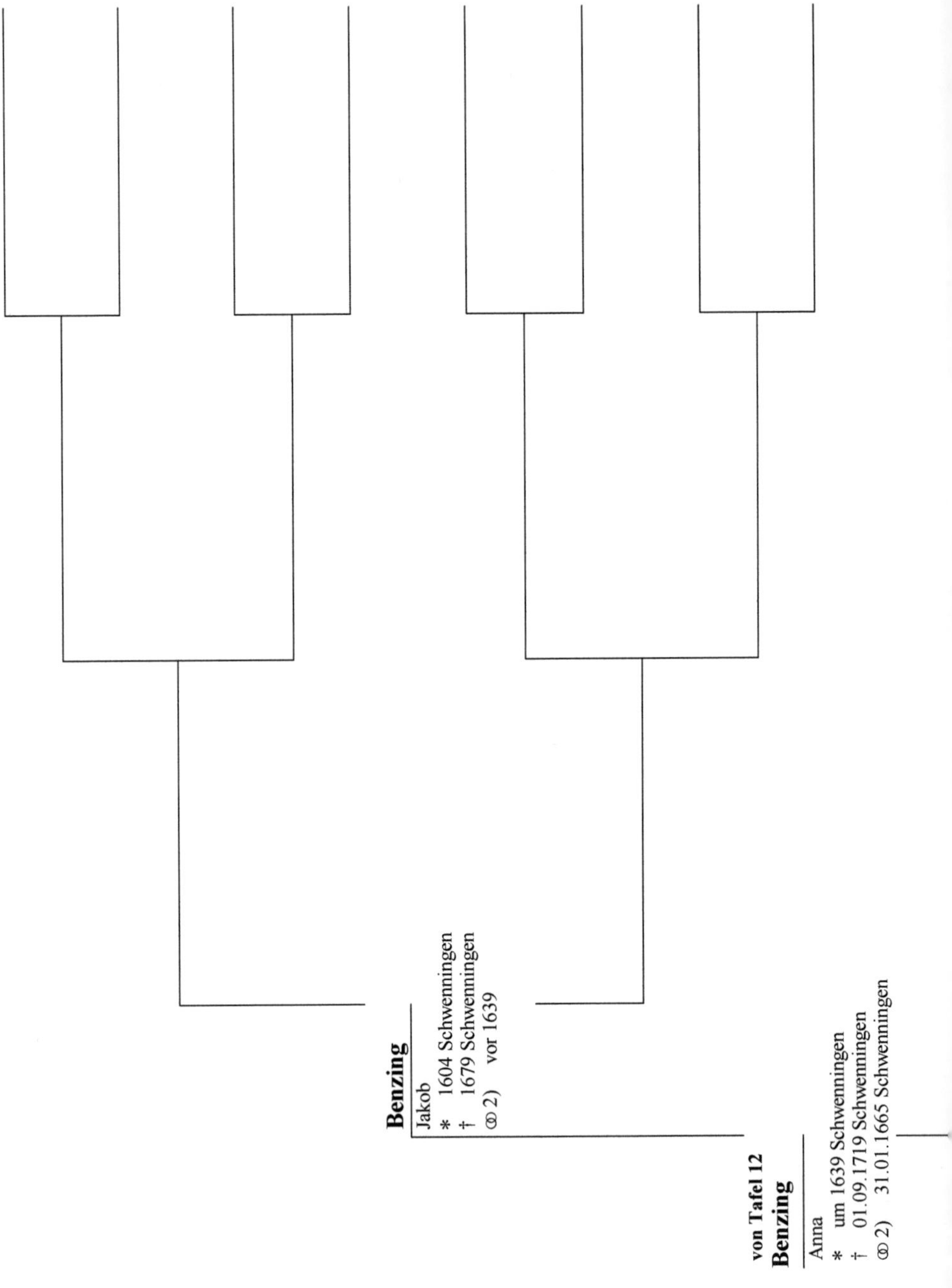

Benzing
Jakob
* 1604 Schwenningen
† 1679 Schwenningen
⚭ 2) vor 1639

von Tafel 12
Benzing
Anna
* um 1639 Schwenningen
† 01.09.1719 Schwenningen
⚭ 2) 31.01.1665 Schwenningen

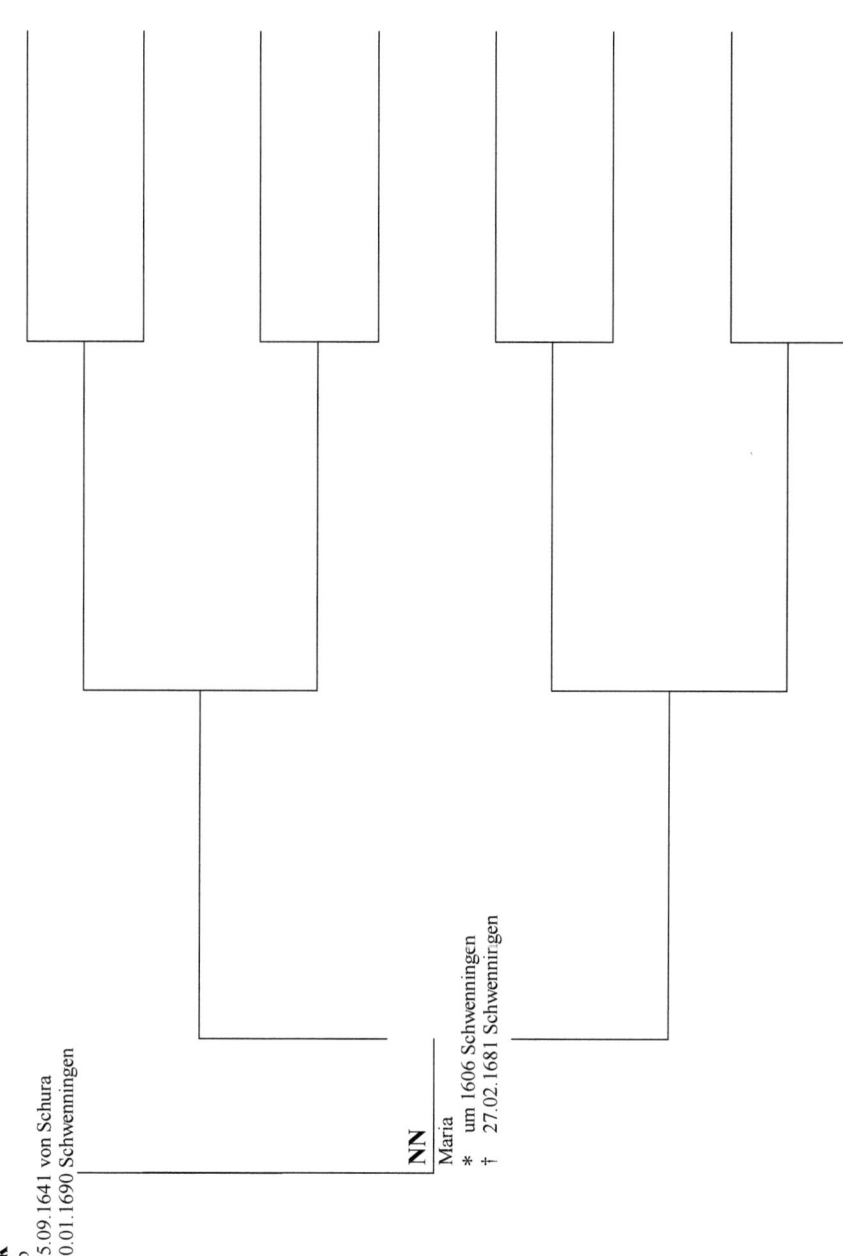

Link
Jakob
* 05.09.1641 von Schura
† 30.01.1690 Schwenningen

NN
Maria
* um 1606 Schwenningen
† 27.02.1681 Schwennirgen

Genealogical table no. 31

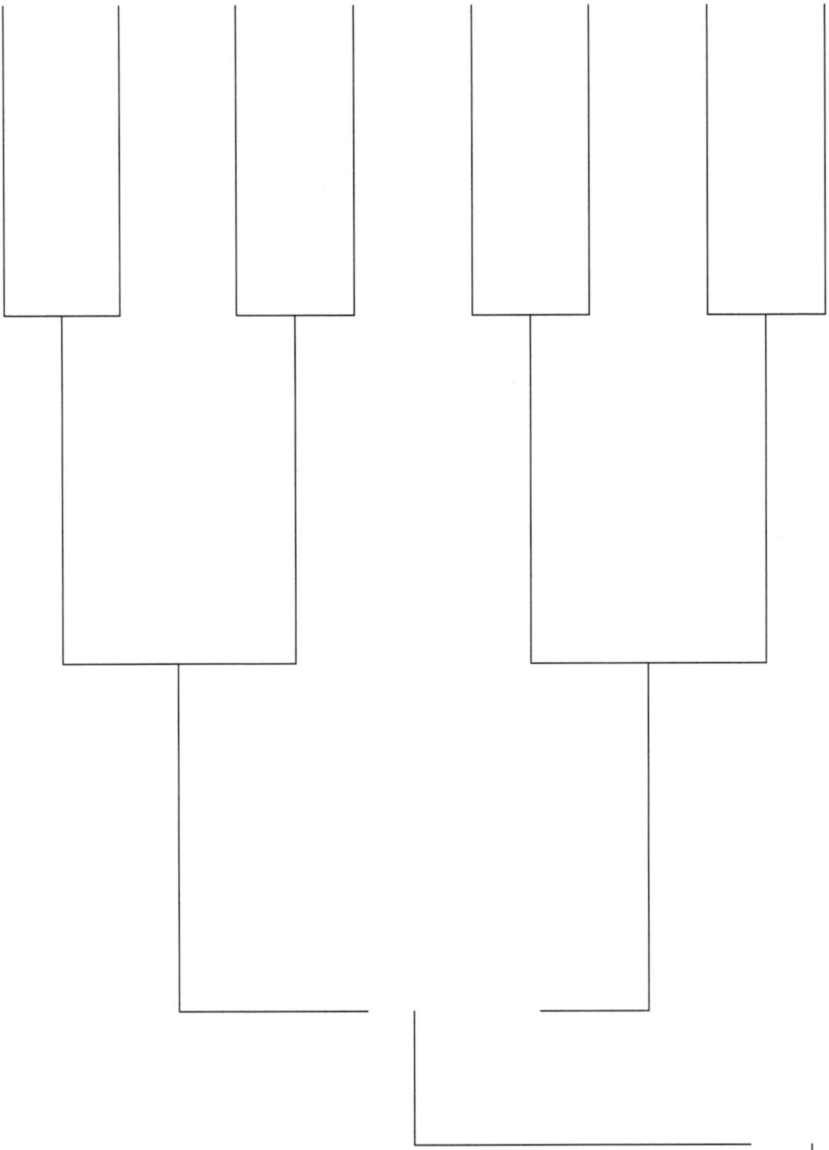

von Tafel 13
Lauffer

Jacob
* um 1622 Schwenningen
† 25.09.1674 Schwenningen
⚭ 16.06.1663 Schwenningen

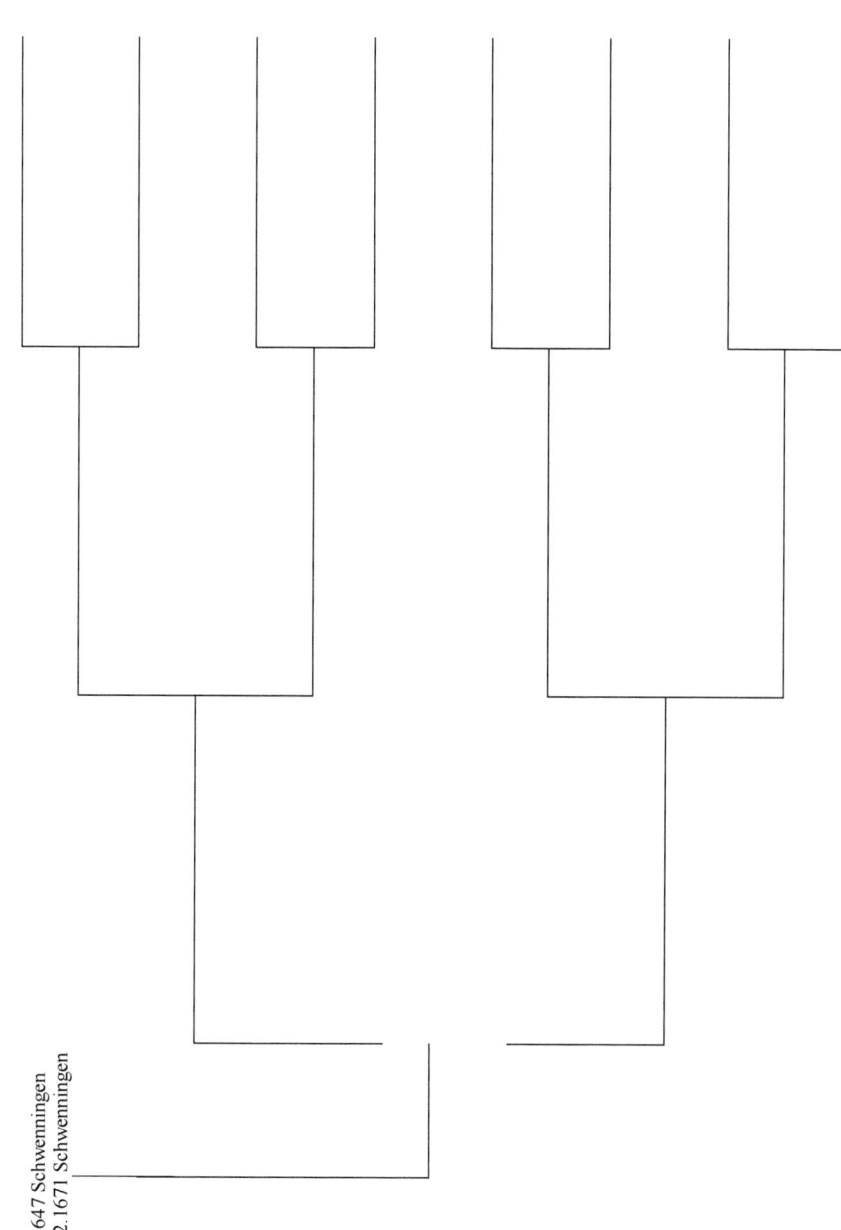

Kaiser
Anna

* um 1647 Schwenningen
† 25.12.1671 Schwenningen

Genealogical table no. 32

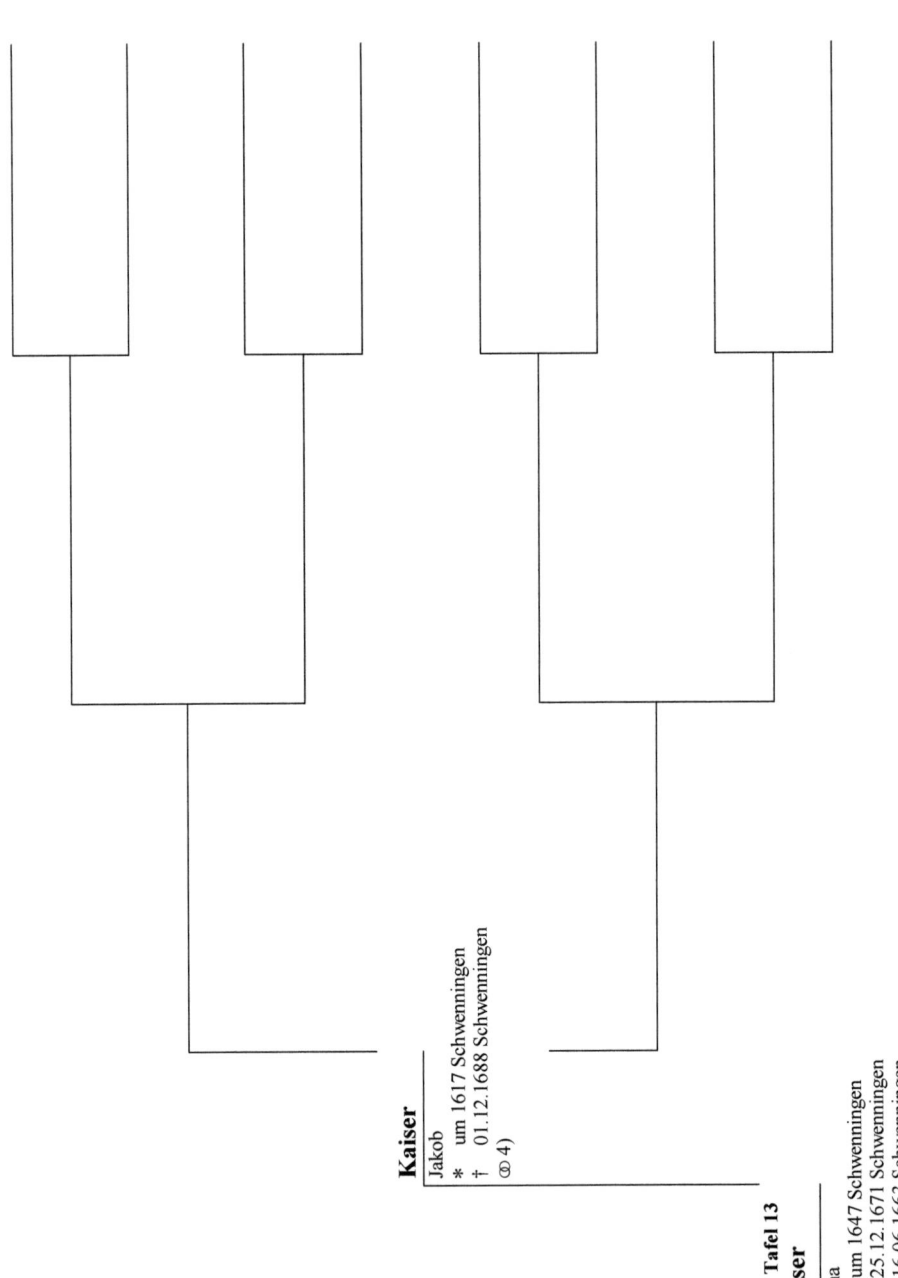

Kaiser
Jakob
* um 1617 Schwenningen
† 01.12.1688 Schwenningen
⚭ 4)

von Tafel 13
Kaiser
Anna
* um 1647 Schwenningen
† 25.12.1671 Schwenningen
⚭ 16.06.1663 Schwenningen

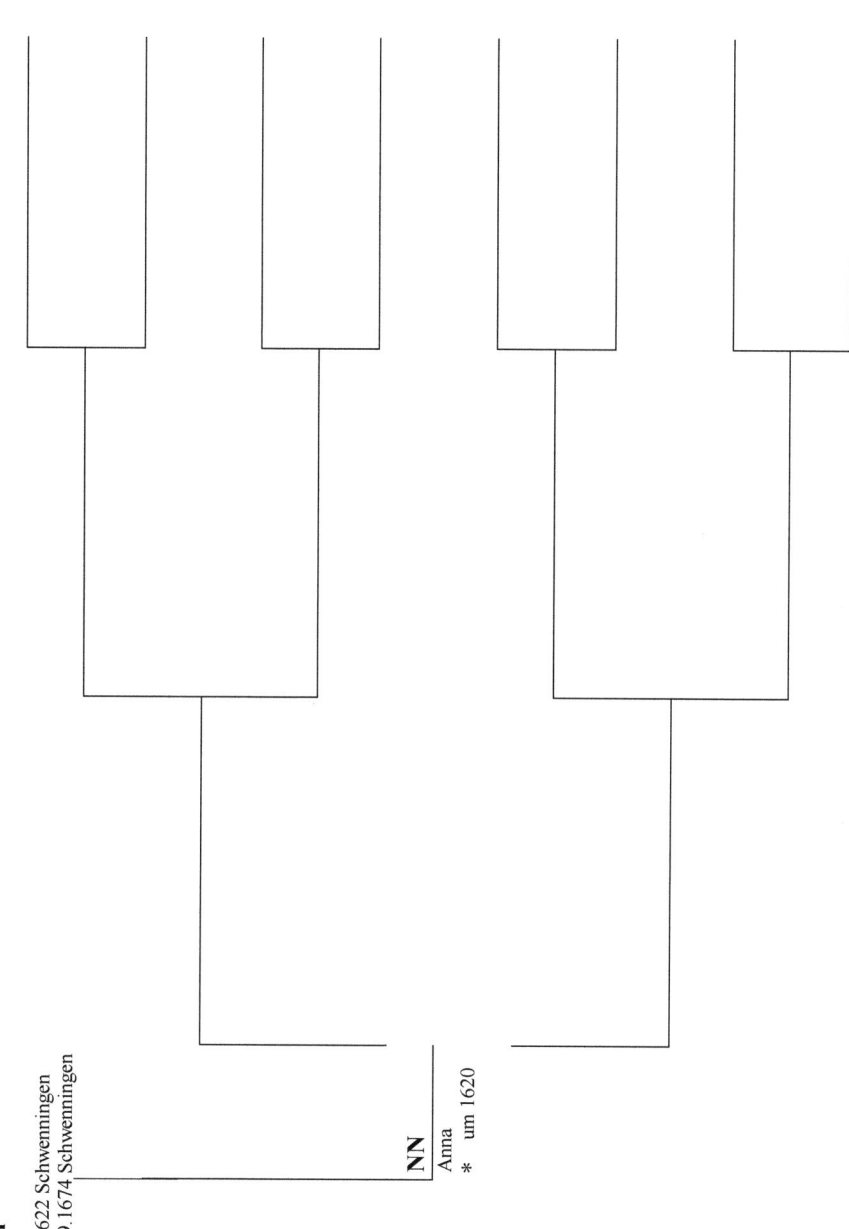

Lauffer
Jacob
* um 1622 Schwenningen
† 25.09.1674 Schwenningen

NN
Anna
* um 1620

Genealogical table no. 33

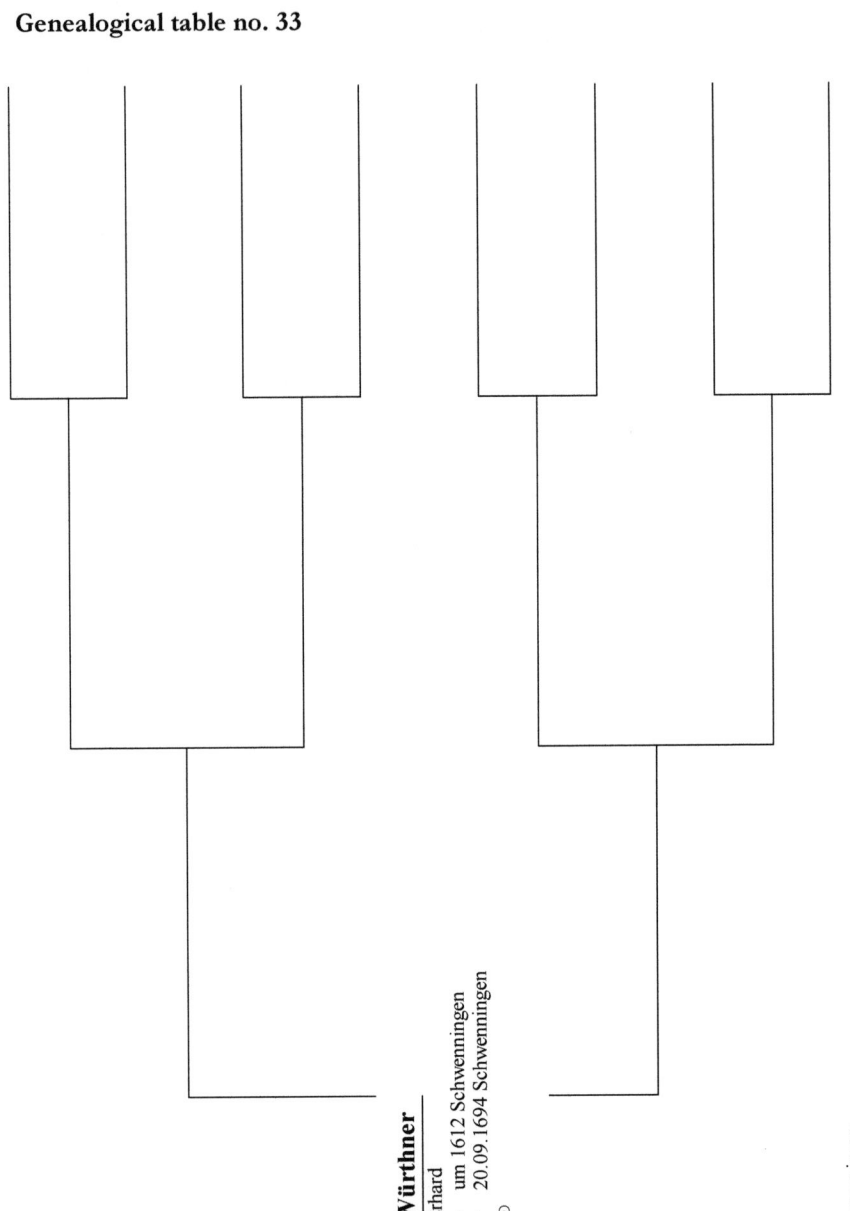

Würthner

Erhard
* um 1612 Schwenningen
† 20.09.1694 Schwenningen
⚭

von Tafel 14
Würthner

Jakob
* um 1645 Schwenningen
† 25.03.1690 Schwenningen
⚭ 2) 02.11.1669 Schwenningen

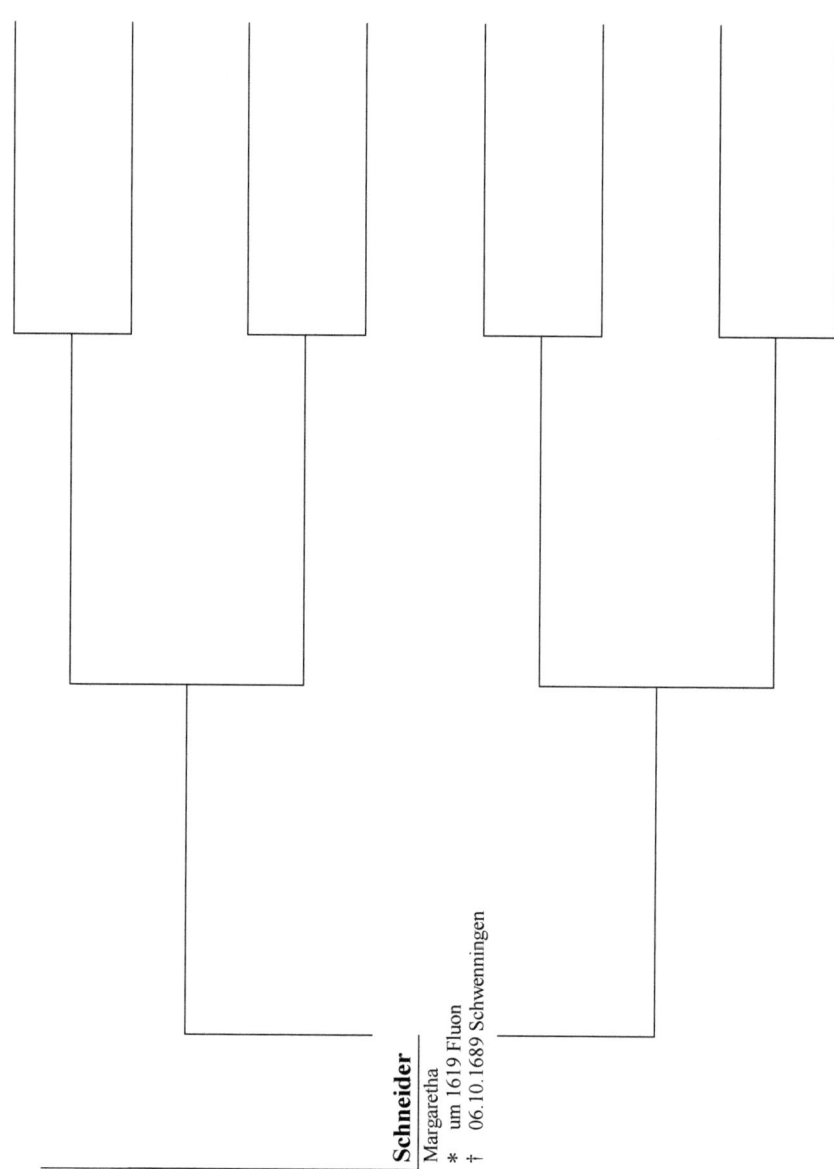

Schneider
Margaretha
* um 1619 Fluon
† 06.10.1689 Schwenningen

Schuler
Katharina
* 1653

Genealogical table no. 34

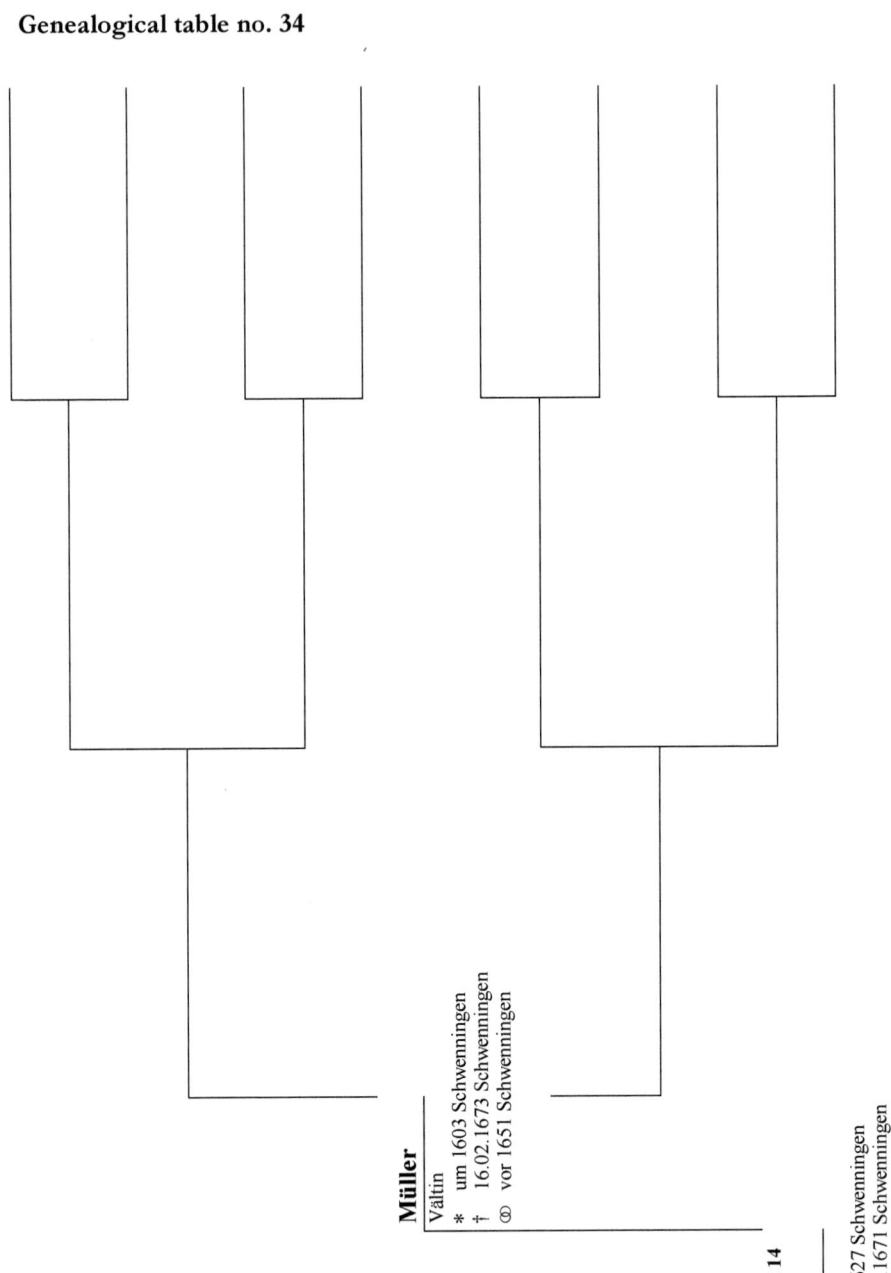

Müller
Vältin
* um 1603 Schwenningen
† 16.02.1673 Schwenningen
⚭ vor 1651 Schwenningen

von Tafel 14
Müller
Barbara
* um 1627 Schwenningen
† 13.10.1671 Schwenningen
⚭ um 1653 Schwenningen

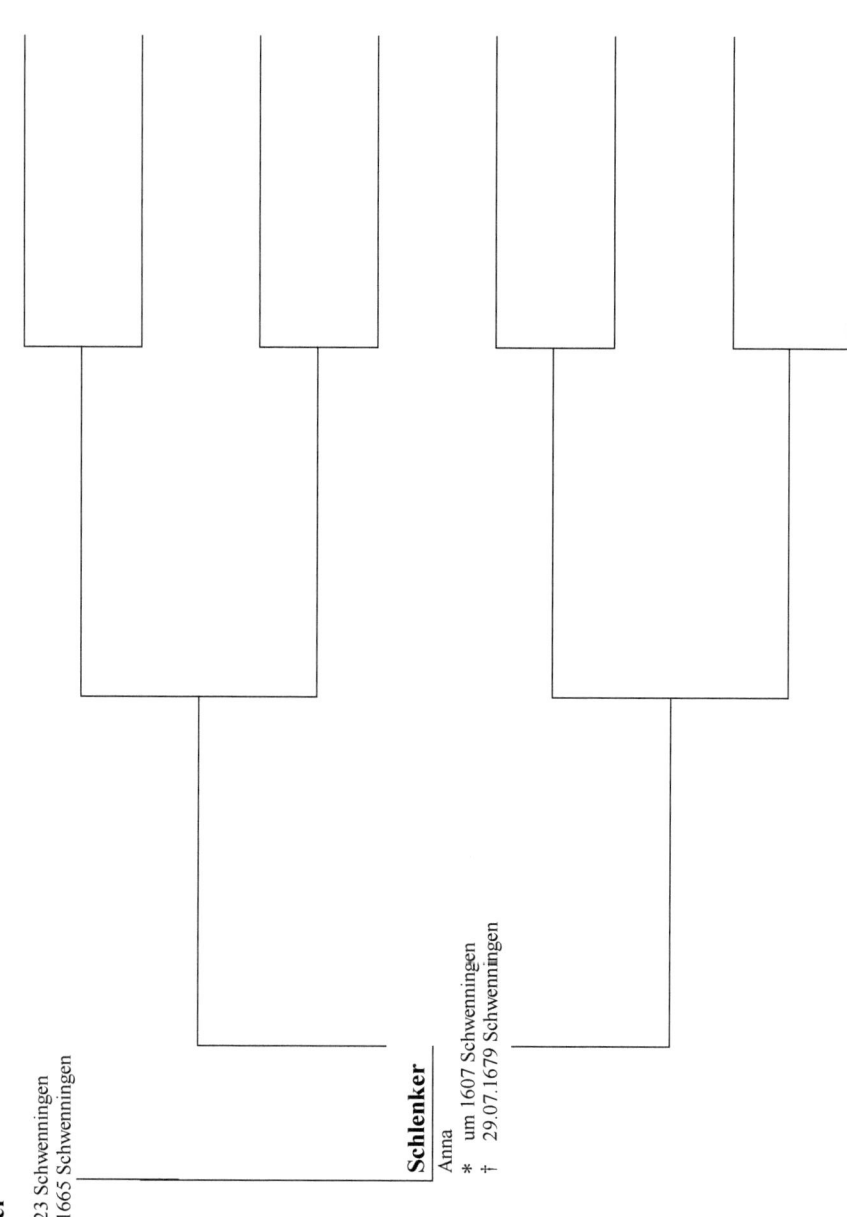

Schlenker
Joseph
* um 1623 Schwenningen
† 17.12.1665 Schwenningen

Schlenker
Anna
* um 1607 Schwenningen
† 29.07.1679 Schwenningen

Genealogical table no. 35

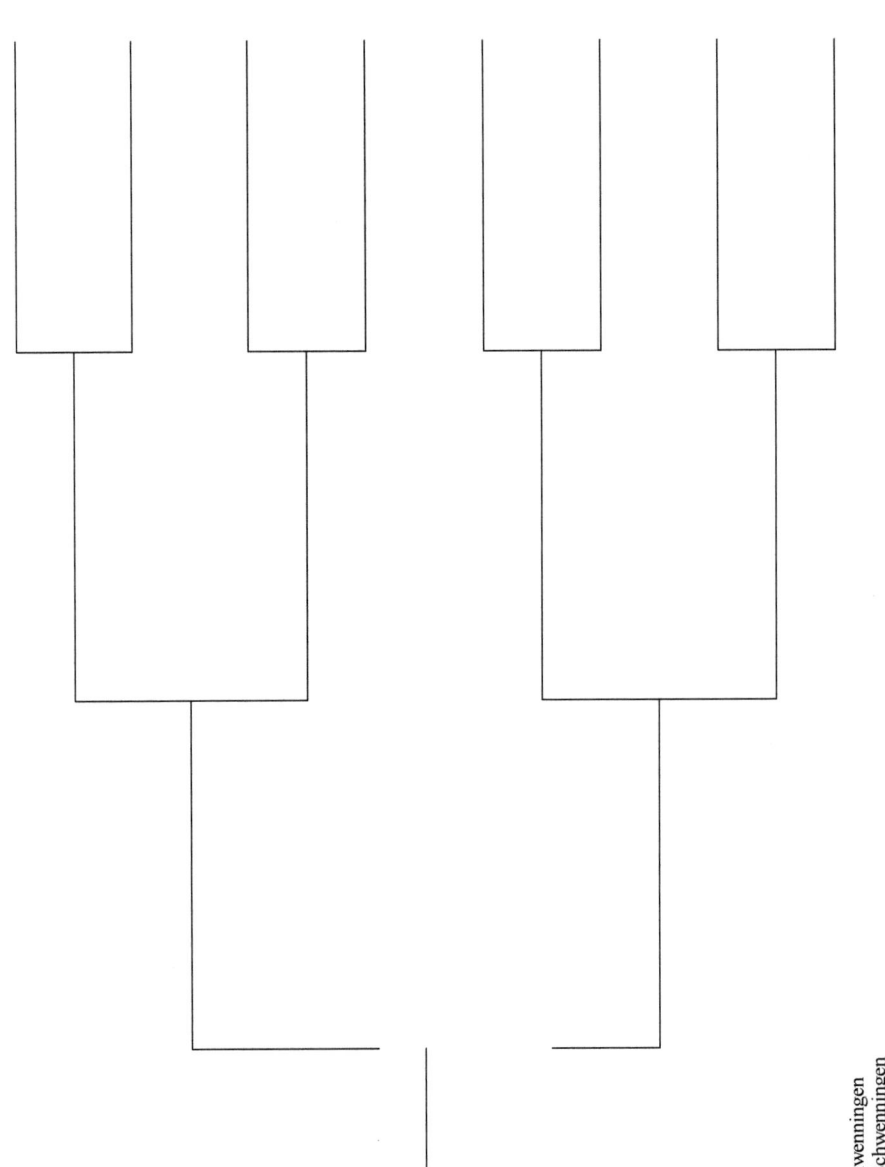

von Tafel 14
Haller

Jakob
* um 1615 Schwenningen
† 17.09.1698 Schwenningen
⚭ 2) um 1640 Schwenningen

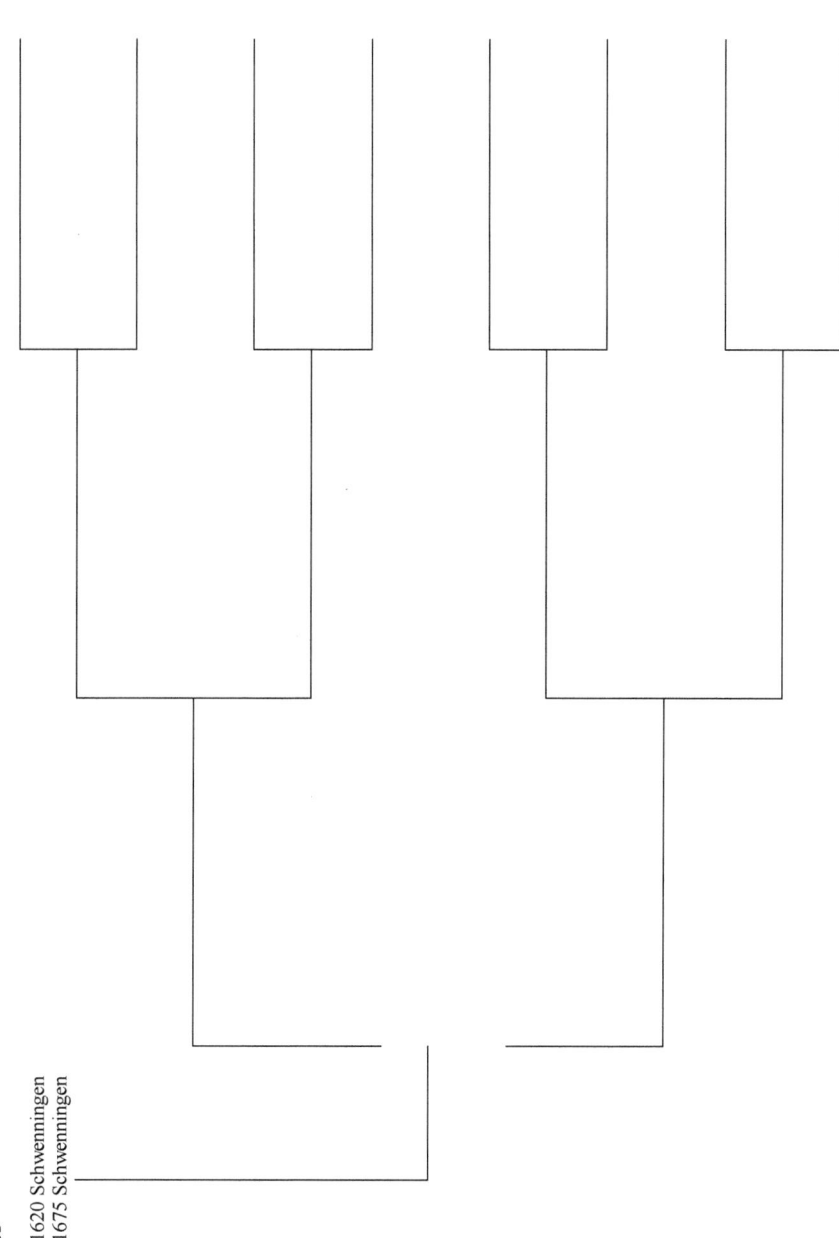

Lauffer
Anna
* um 1620 Schwenningen
† um 1675 Schwenningen

Genealogical table no. 36

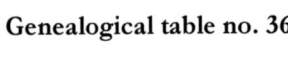

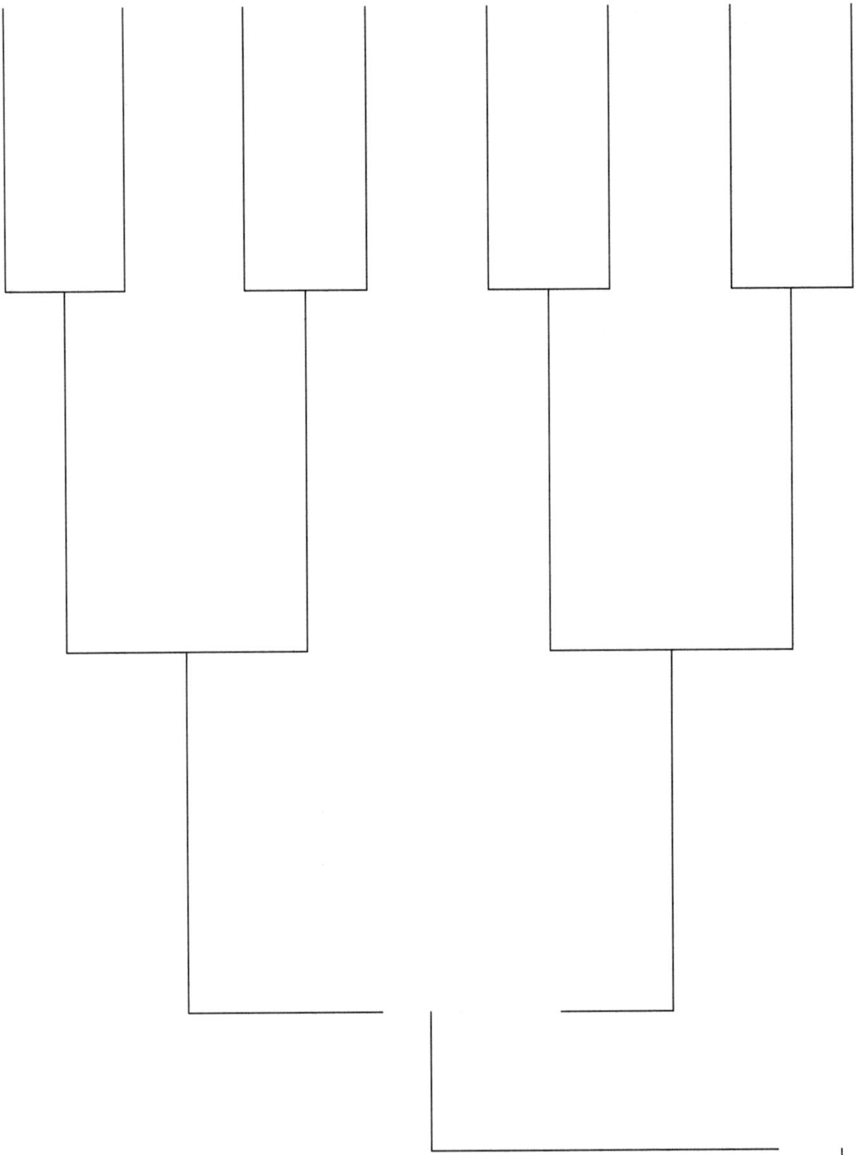

von Tafel 14
Haller

Jakob
* um 1615 Schwenningen
† 17.09.1698 Schwenningen
⚭ 2) um 1640 Schwenningen

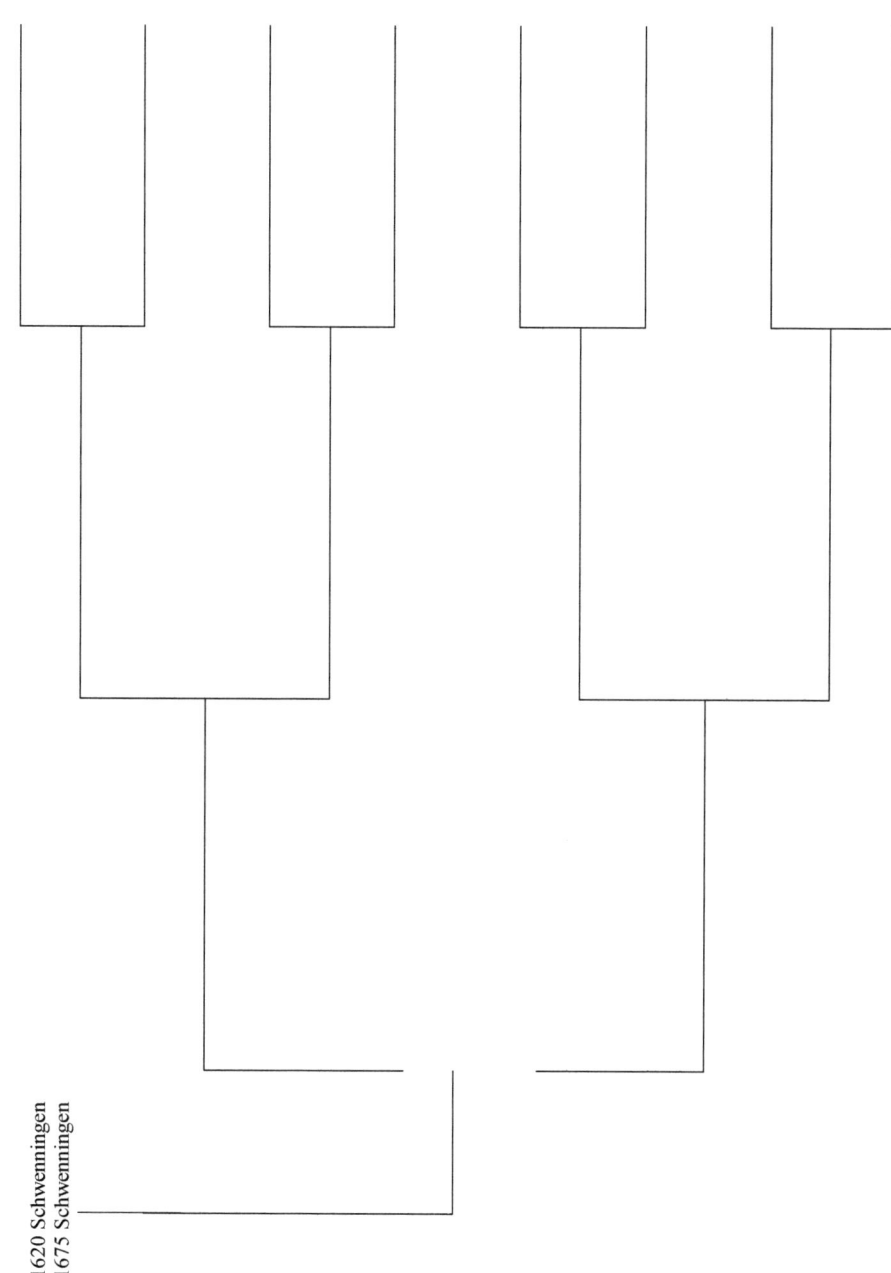

Lauffer

Anna

* um 1620 Schwenningen

† um 1675 Schwenningen

Genealogical table no. 37

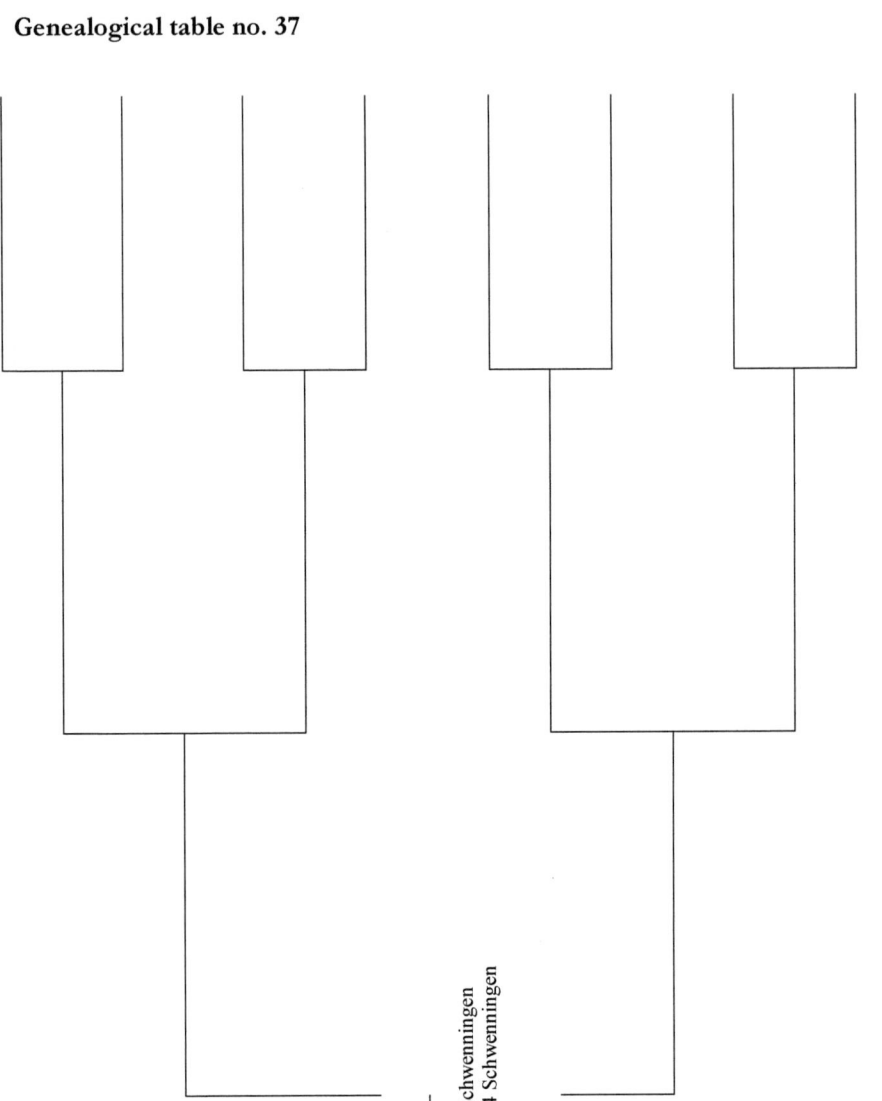

Würthner

Erhard

* um 1612 Schwenningen

† 20.09.1694 Schwenningen

∞

von Tafel 14

Würthner

Jakob

* um 1645 Schwenningen

† 25.03.1690 Schwenningen

∞ 02.11.1669 Schwenningen

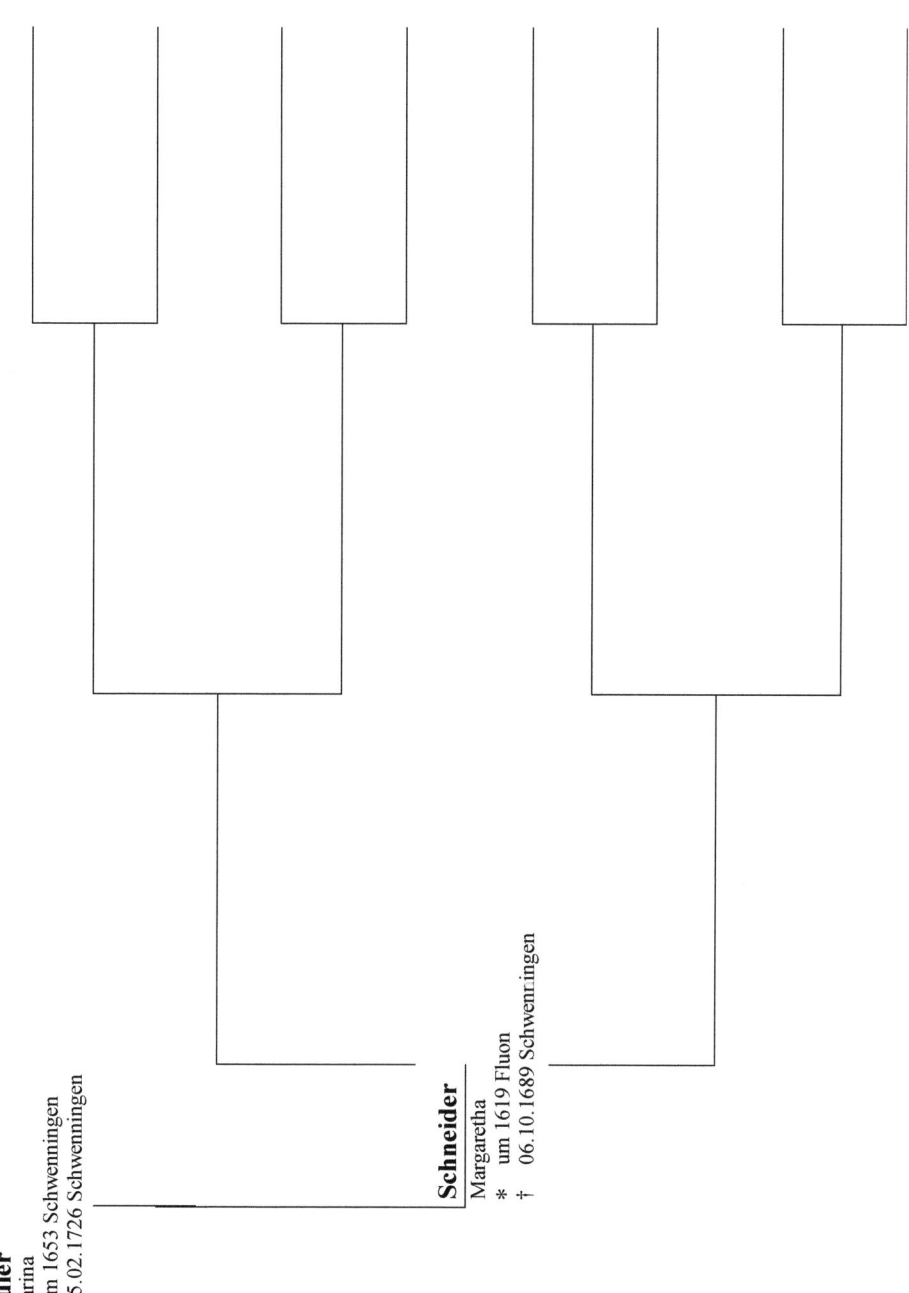

Schuler
Catharina
* um 1653 Schwenningen
† 15.02.1726 Schwenningen

Schneider
Margaretha
* um 1619 Fluon
† 06.10.1689 Schwenningen

Genealogical table no. 38

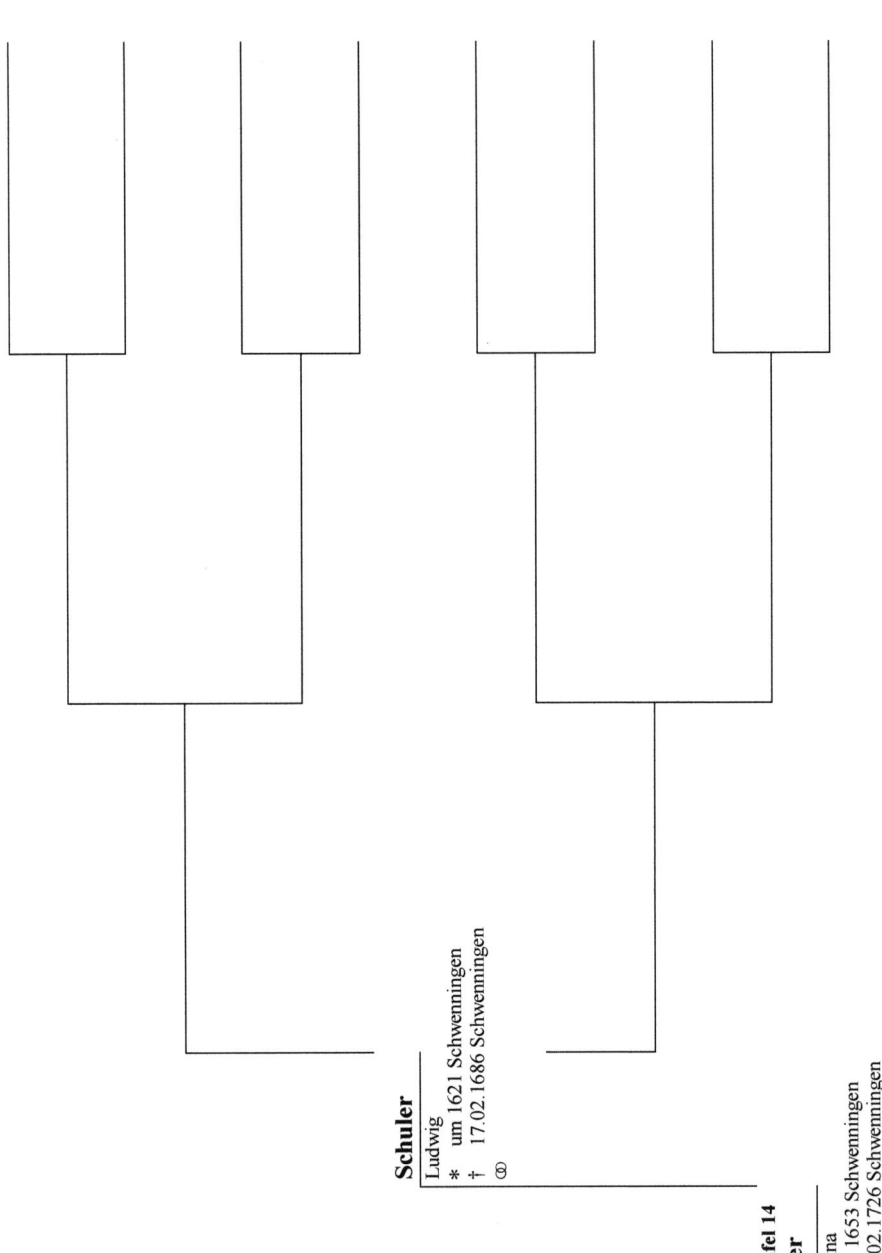

Schuler
Ludwig
* um 1621 Schwenningen
† 17.02.1686 Schwenningen
⚭

von Tafel 14
Schuler
Catharina
* um 1653 Schwenningen
† 15.02.1726 Schwenningen
⚭ 02.11.1669 Schwenningen

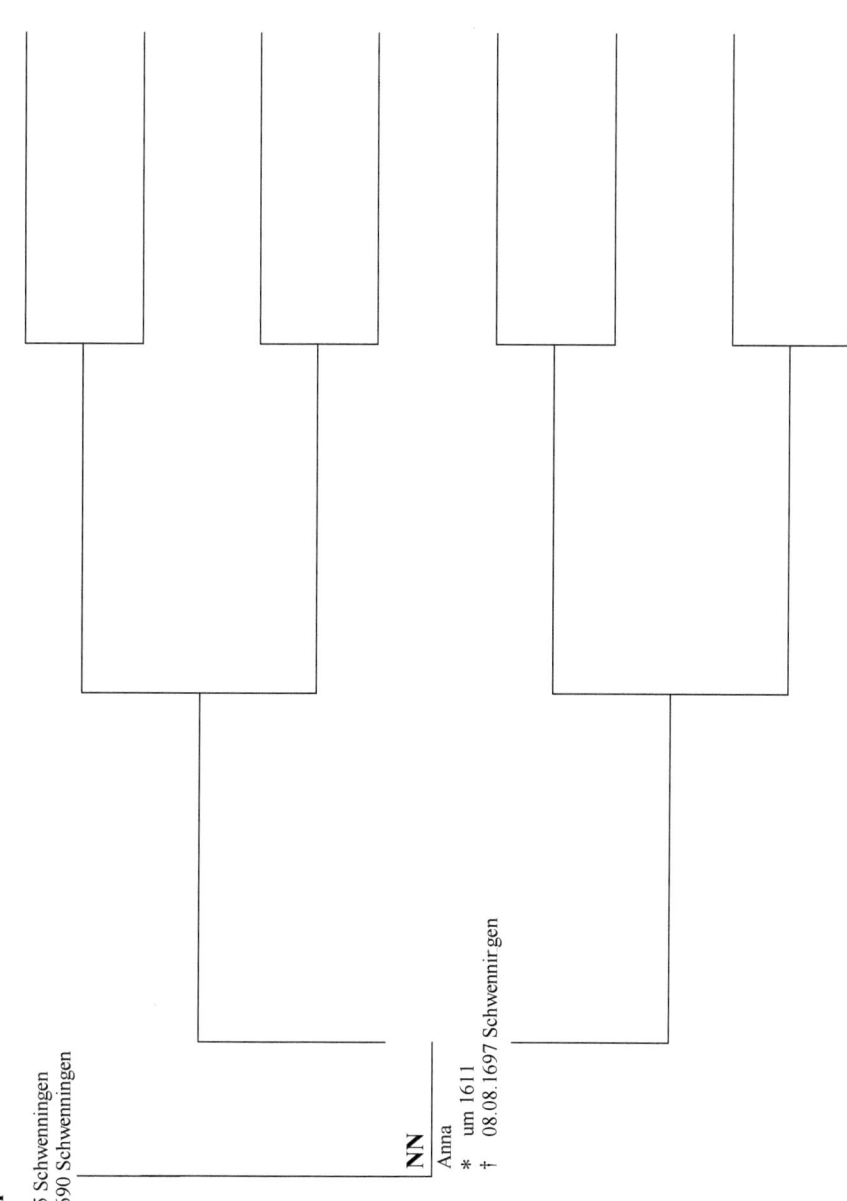

Würthner
Jakob
* um 1645 Schwenningen
† 25.03.1690 Schwenningen

NN
Anna
* um 1611
† 08.08.1697 Schwennirgen

Genealogical table no. 39

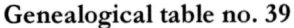

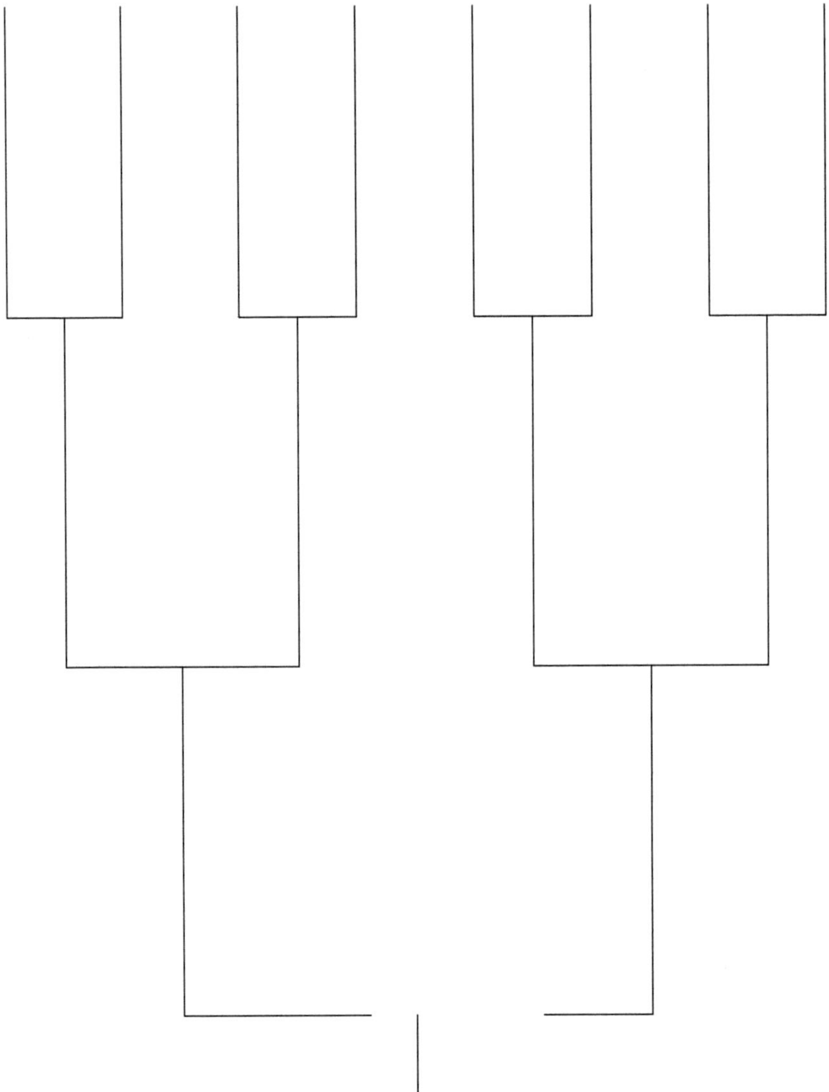

von Tafel 15
Lauffer

Jacob
* um 1622 Schwenningen
† 25.09.1674 Schwenningen
⚭ 16.06.1663 Schwenningen

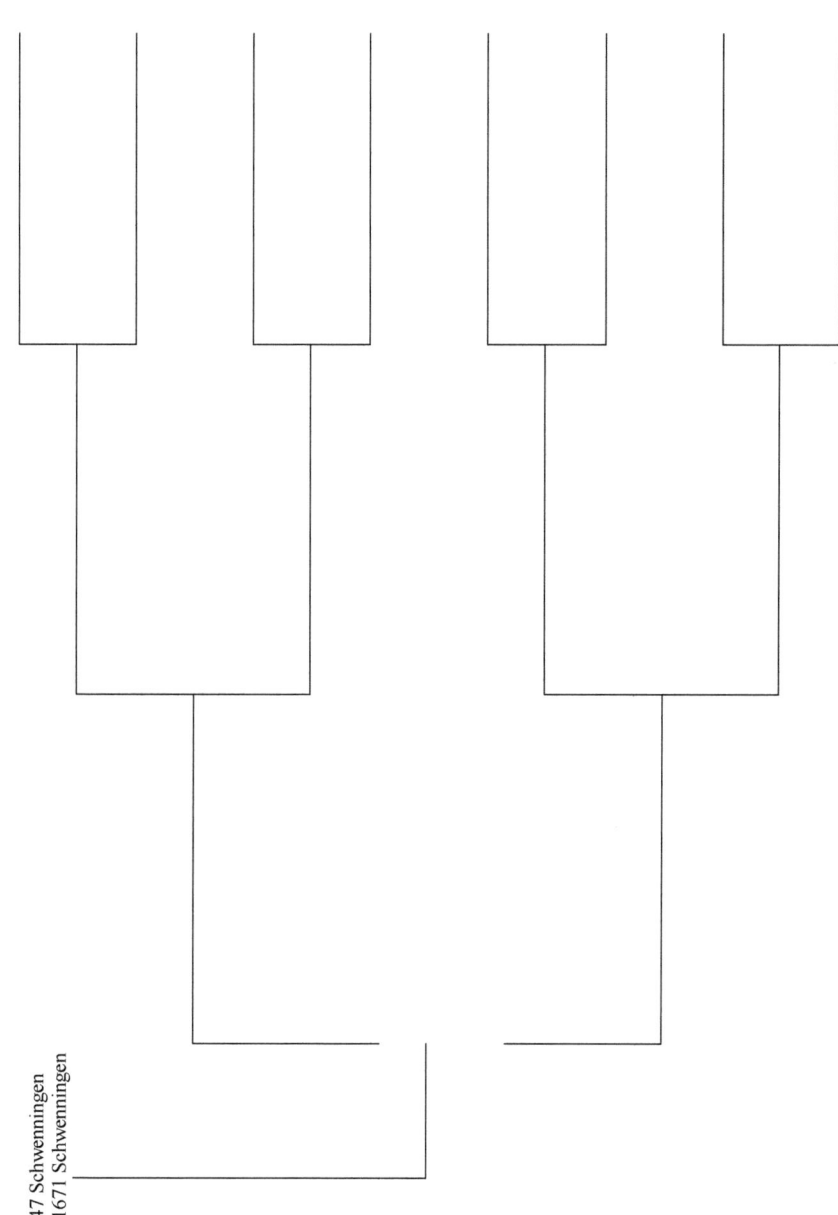

Kaiser
Anna
* um 1647 Schwenningen
† 25.12.1671 Schwenningen

Genealogical table no. 40

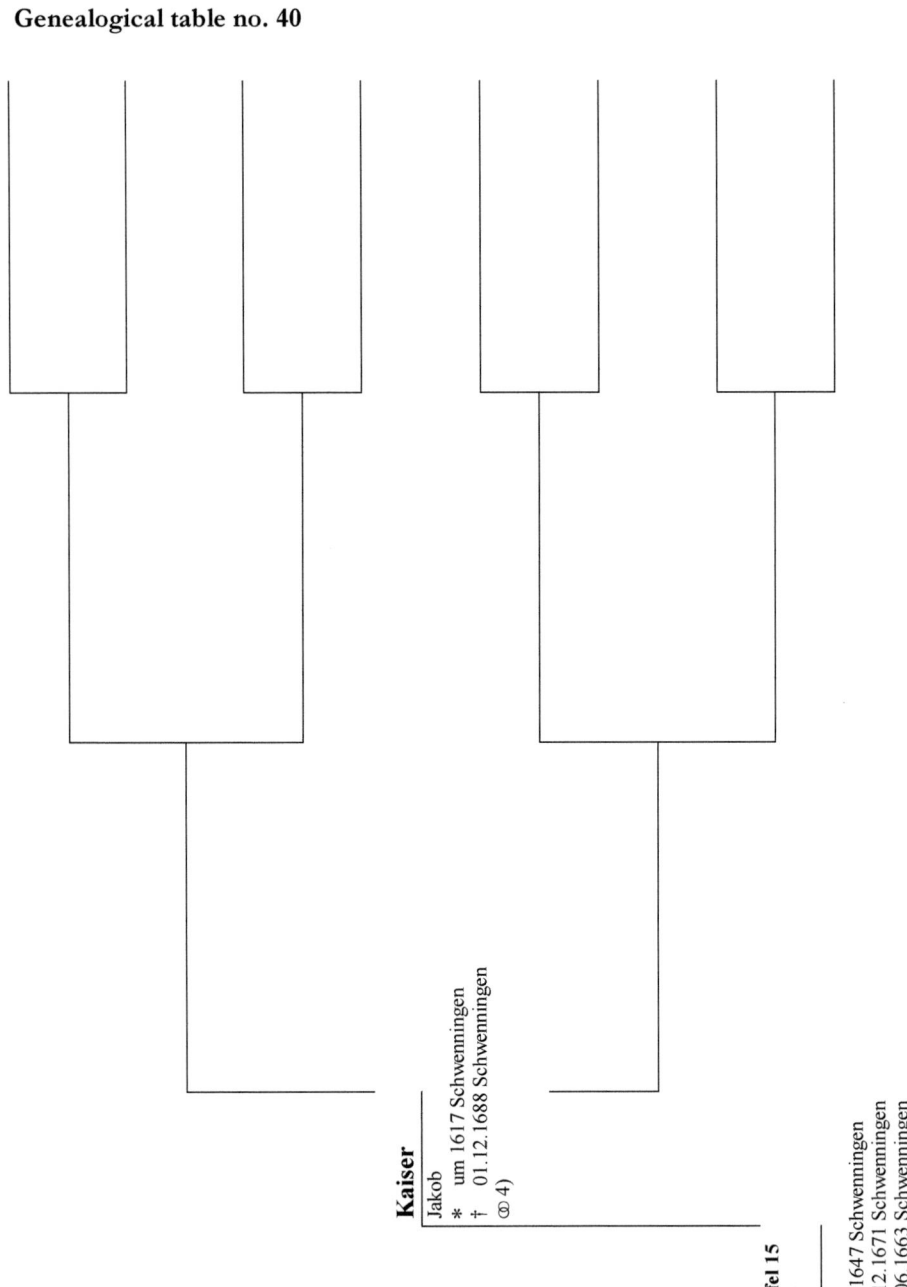

Kaiser
Jakob
* um 1617 Schwenningen
† 01.12.1688 Schwenningen
⚭ 4)

von Tafel 15
Kaiser
Anna
* um 1647 Schwenningen
† 25.12.1671 Schwenningen
⚭ 16.06.1663 Schwenningen

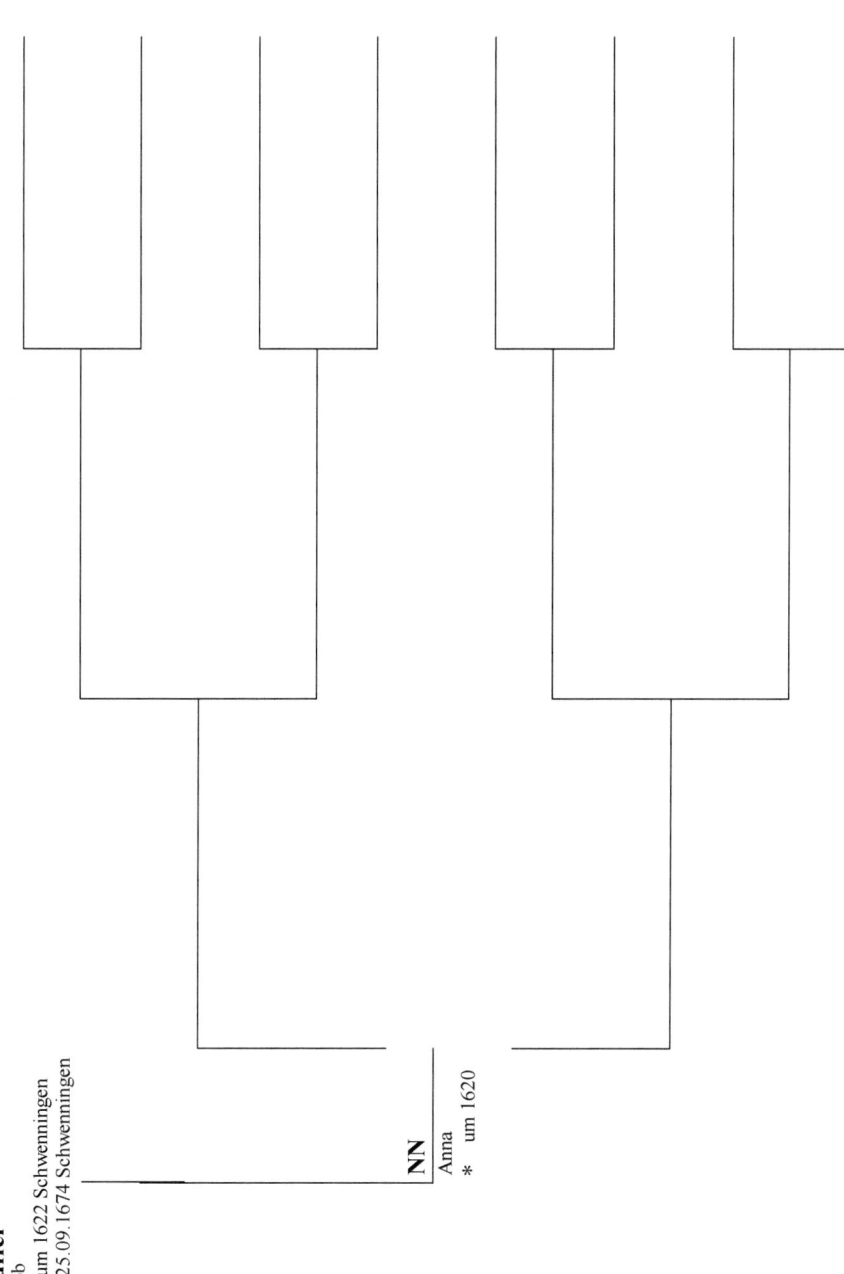

Lauffer
Jacob
* um 1622 Schwenningen
† 25.09.1674 Schwenningen

NN
Anna
* um 1620

Register of Schwenningen Family Tree Names

Beate Adomeit

Name	Family tree table no.
Benzing, Agatha, * um 1600	8
Benzing, Agatha, * 07.02.1653	2, 4, 19, 20
Benzing, Anna, * um 1639	3, 12, 29, 30
Benzing, Anna, * 18.11.1730	1-3
Benzing, Christian, * um 1620	2-3, 20
Benzing, Christian, * 17.02.1660	16
Benzing, Christian, * 18.09.1680	3
Benzing, Christian, * 05.03.1691	16
Benzing, Christian, * 16.12.1714	16
Benzing, Eva Christina, * 13.03.1740	16
Benzing, Hans Martin, * 17.02.1704	3
Benzing, Jakob, * 1604	3, 5, 11, 14, 30
Benzing, Johannes (Hanß), * um 1646	3
Benzing, Katharina, * 02.02.1655	5, 11, 14
Benzing, Margaretha, * 24.02.1654	16
Biedermann, Hannß, * um 1621	3, 7
Biedermann, Jakob, * um 1621	3, 7
Biedermann, Hannß, * 06.01.1660	3, 7
Biedermann, Maria, * 08.10.1686	2
Boper, Hans, * um 1620	2
Boppin, Regula, * um 1647	8
Fuckher, Conrad, * um 1600	8
Fuckher, Maria, * um 1627	10, 13, 15
Glaser, Maria, * um 1623	8
Glunz, Maria, * um 1600	9
Götz, Maria, * um 1705	10
Hackenjos, Maraia, * um 1637	10
Haller, Barbara, * 24.08.1684	16
Haller, Christina, * um 1662	6, 10, 14, 25, 36
Haller, Jakob, * um 1615	16
Haller, Jakob, * um 1640	10
Haller, Konrad, * um 1641	10
Haller, Maria, * 02.04.1657	6, 14
Haller, Walburga, * 23.03.1655	1
Hanßmann, Anna Maria, * 09.10.1767	1, 8
Hanßmann, Martin, *	3, 7, 24